C000165042

The
WISDOM
of the
ANCIENT GREEKS

TITLES IN THIS SERIES

The Wisdom of the Arabs, ISBN 1–85168–283–X

The Wisdom of Buddhism, ISBN 1–85168–226–0

The Wisdom of the Confucians, ISBN 1–85168–259–7

The Wisdom of Hinduism, ISBN 1–85168–227–9

The Wisdom of Jesus, ISBN 1–85168–225–2

The Wisdom of Judaism, ISBN 1–85168–228–7

The Wisdom of the Kabbalah, ISBN 1–85168–297–X

The Wisdom of the Qur'an, ISBN 1–85168–224–4

The Wisdom of Sikhism, ISBN 1–85168–280–5

The Wisdom of Sufism, ISBN 1–85168–260–0

The Wisdom of the Tao, ISBN 1–85168–232–5

The Wisdom of Zen, ISBN 1–85168–281–3

The
WISDOM
of the
ANCIENT GREEKS

Compiled by
Mel Thompson

ONEWORLD

OXFORD

THE WISDOM OF THE ANCIENT GREEKS

Oneworld Publications
(Sales and Editorial)
185 Banbury Road
Oxford OX2 7AR
England
www.oneworld-publications.com

© Oneworld 2002

ISBN 1–85168–298–8

Cover and text design by Design Deluxe
Typeset by Cyclops Media Productions
Printed and bound by Graphicom Srl, Vicenza, Italy

CONTENTS

PREFACE

IT IS quite impossible to sum up in a few words the enormous wealth of epic poetry, drama and philosophy that has come down to us from Ancient Greece. It has provided inspiration for both rational thought and artistic creativity from one generation to the next within Western culture.

The wisdom of Ancient Greece combined passion, a raw appreciation of human emotions and the tragedy of a life driven by them, with the most rigorous and careful analysis of ideas. Greek drama probed every recess of human frailty, exposing the agony of self-doubt and the sense of injustice in the world, and in doing so elevated language as never before. That wisdom was also the source of science, philosophy, psychology and politics as we know them today, and the language in which we explore these subjects depends to a great extent on Greek terms.

The passages included in this anthology can therefore represent no more than a personal choice, selected from this vast literature. Whether poetry, drama or philosophy, they seek to address the key issues of human life and death, its meaning and its place within the universe.

Those who explore the art and literature of Ancient Greece and set them within the context of Western culture, tend to resort to superlatives, for it is difficult to overestimate the achievements of that period. Below you will find just a few such comments, included here to set the context for the passages of wisdom that follow.

HE CAME at the end of the creative period in Greek thought, and after his death it was two thousand years before the world produced any philosopher who could be regarded as approximately his equal.

BERTRAND RUSSELL on Aristotle, *History of Western Philosophy*

THESE DIALOGUES are among the world's great literature. In addition to containing some of the best philosophy ever produced they are beautifully written – many language scholars think they contain the finest of all Greek prose.

BRYAN MAGEE on Plato's *Dialogues*, *The Story of Philosophy*

THE ANCIENT philosophers created and laid much of the groundwork for later philosophical debate in the fields of ontology, epistemology, logic, ethics and political philosophy. They also established the crucial features of philosophical method – open-mindedness about the agenda of problems, and rational progress through argument and debate.

J. D. G. EVANS, *The Oxford Companion to Philosophy*

THE PERSON of Socrates became, and has remained ever since, so powerful an icon for the life of moral scrutiny that it is his name that is used to mark this watershed in the history of philosophy. In the century or so that followed his death, many schools looked back to him as the living embodiment of philosophy and sought the principles of his life and thought in philosophical theory.

A. J. BAKER, *The Concise Routledge Encyclopedia of Philosophy*

ALMOST EVERYTHING about Homer is debatable, except the centrality to ancient Greek culture of the two epics connected with his name, the *Iliad* and the *Odyssey*, and thus their importance for Western civilisation as a whole … The sophistication and polish of the writing gave the Homeric narratives universal appeal. They remained part of the Greek consciousness throughout Greek history, and have retained their appeal today. One reason for this is that their focus of interest is always human. The Olympian gods, when they appear, are treated as beings with distinctly human frailties – they are often less admirable than the men and women whose fates they govern. Human beings, by contrast, are enlarged rather than diminished, even when they are shown behaving badly.

EDWARD LUCIE-SMITH, *Art and Civilisation*

FROM A period of about 200 years, beginning in the late 500s BC, Athens was the centre of Greek culture. The height of this period, from 461 BC to 431 BC, is often called the Golden Age. During this period, largely as a result of the emergence of democracy, literature flourished. Drama in the form of tragedy became the most important literary form. Aeschylus, Sophocles and Euripides are the three greatest tragic playwrights. Aeschylus's plays are noted for seriousness, majestic language and complexity of thought. Those of Sophocles are noted for characterisation, graceful language, and sense of proportion. Euripides, the 'philosopher of the stage' explored human emotions and passions. Comedy was also prominent in the 400s BC. The plays of Aristophanes, a writer of bawdy and satiric comedy, reflected the sense of freedom, vitality, and spirit that pervaded Athens at the time.

The New Webster's International Encyclopedia

DATES OF SOME KEY WRITERS INCLUDED IN THIS ANTHOLOGY

Homer	c. eighth century BC
Aesop	sixth century BC
Aeschylus	525–456 BC
Sophocles	496–405 BC
Protagoras	c. 490–c. 420 BC
Euripides	c. 480–406 BC
Socrates	454–399 BC
Aristophanes	450–386 BC
Plato	427–347 BC
Aristotle	384–322 BC
Epicurus	341–271 BC
Cynics	from mid-fourth century BC
Epictetus	c. 50–c. 120 CE
Plotinus	204–270 CE

WISDOM, PHILOSOPHY
AND LEARNING

Why, my good sir, must not the wisest appear more beautiful?

PLATO, *Protagoras (310)*

P HILOSOPHY DOES not promise to secure for a man any external thing. If it did, it would take on something outside its proper subject-matter. For as wood is the material of the carpenter, and bronze that of the sculptor, so the subject-matter of the art of life is each person's own life.

EPICTETUS, *Discourses I, chapter 15*

I F THE intellect is divine compared with man, the life of the intellect must be divine compared with the life of a human being. And we ought not to listen to those who warn us that 'man should think the thoughts of man', or 'mortal thoughts fit mortal minds'; but we ought, so far as in us lies, to put on immortality, and to do all that we can to live in conformity with the highest that is in us; for even if it is small in bulk, in power and preciousness it far excels all the rest. Indeed it would seem that this is the true self of the individual, since it is the authoritative and better part of him.

ARISTOTLE, *Ethics, Book 10*

The danger of too much philosophy

FOR PHILOSOPHY, you know, Socrates, is a charming thing, if a man has to do with it moderately in his younger days; but if he continues to spend his time on it too long, it is ruin to any man. However well endowed one may be, if one philosophises far on into life, one must needs find oneself ignorant of everything that ought to be familiar to the man who would be a thorough gentleman and make a good figure in the world. For such people are shown to be ignorant of the laws of their city, and of the terms which have to be used in negotiating agreements with their fellows in private or in public affairs, and of human pleasures and desires; and, in short, to be utterly inexperienced of men's characters. So when they enter upon any private or public business they make themselves ridiculous, just as on the other hand, I suppose, when public men engage in your studies and discussions, they are quite ridiculous.

PLATO, *Gorgias (486)* from an argument of Callicles

※ ΑΡΙΣΤΌΛΗΣ ※

Imago hæc Aristotelis Physicorum &c. libros scribentis, pertinet ad I.

To know is to remember ...

SEEING THEN that the <u>soul is immortal</u> and has been born many times, and has beheld all things both in this world and in the nether realms, she has acquired knowledge of all and everything; so that it is no wonder that she should be able to recollect all that she knew before about virtue and other things. For as all nature is akin, and the soul has learned all things, there is no reason why we should not, by remembering but one single thing – an act which men call learning – discover everything else, if we have courage and faint not in the search; since, it would seem, research and learning are wholly recollection.

PLATO, *Meno (81D)*

MUCH UNDILUTED wine is an enemy of properly performing one's duties. For it confounds one's mind, in which man's ability to reason is situated. It is not easy for the person who strives for great things to accomplish what he attempts unless he enters upon <u>a sober and careful life</u>.

ANACHARSIS (a Cynic)

'SOBER + CAREFUL'

Never too late to learn ...

PERHAPS YOU will allow me to give you a piece of advice. I tell you, gentlemen – and this is confidential – that we ought all alike to seek out the best teacher we can find, first for ourselves – for we need one – and then for our boys, sparing neither expense nor anything else we can do: but to leave ourselves as we now are, this I do not advise. And if anyone makes fun of us for seeing fit to go to school at our time of life, I think we should appeal to Homer, who said that 'shame is no good mate for the needy man'. So let us not mind what anyone may say, but join together in arranging for our own and the boys' tuition.

PLATO, *Larches (201B)*

IN A philosophical debate, he gains most who is defeated, since he learns most.

EPICURUS

On education   [WHAT IS EDUCATION FOR?]

FOR IN modern times there are opposing views about the tasks to be set, for there are no generally accepted assumptions about what the young should learn, either of virtue or for the best life; nor yet is it clear whether their education ought to be conducted with more concern for the intellect than for the character of the soul. The problem has been complicated by the education we see actually given; and it is by no means certain whether training should be directed at things useful in life, or at those conducive to virtue, or at exceptional accomplishments.

ARISTOTLE, *Politics, Book VIII, ii*

On debating theses

'ATTACK'

To DEFEND either a thesis or a definition, you should first work out an attack on it for yourself. For it is clear that it is those things on the basis of which questioners refute the theses that you should oppose.

'UNACCEPTABLE THESIS'

Avoid defending an unacceptable thesis. ('Unacceptable' could have two meanings: it might mean either a thesis from which absurdities follow, e.g. if someone were to say that all things move or that nothing does; or, it might mean what a bad character would choose and what is contrary to our wishes, e.g. that pleasure is the good or that doing wrong is better than suffering it.) For people will take you to be saying what you think, not defending something for the sake of argument, and hate you.

ARISTOTLE, *Topics*, Book 8, *chapter 9*

Iᴺ ᴛʜᴇ world of knowledge, the last thing to be perceived and only with great difficulty is the essential Form of Goodness. Once it is perceived, the conclusion must follow that, for all things, this is the cause of whatever is right and good; in the visible world it gives birth to light and to the lord of light, while it is itself sovereign in the intelligible world and the parent of intelligence and truth. Without having had a vision of this Form no one can act with wisdom, either in his own life or in matters of state.

PLATO, *The Republic, Book XXV*

Aɴᴅ ɪᴛ will be the business of reason to rule with wisdom and forethought on behalf of the entire soul; while the spirited element ought to act as its subordinate ally. The two will be brought into accord … by that combination of mental and bodily training which will tune up one string of the instrument and relax the other, nourishing the reasoning part on the study of noble literature and allaying the other's wildness by harmony and rhythm.

PLATO, *The Republic, Book XIV*

Perception and reality

IT IS not things in themselves that trouble us, but our opinions of things.

EPICTETUS

On being wise   [BREAKING OVER IGNORANCE]

CHAEREPHON went to Delphi and boldly asked the oracle to tell him ... whether anyone was wiser than I (Socrates) was, and the Pythian prophetess answered that there was no man wiser ... Why do I mention this? Because I am going to explain to you why I have such an evil name. When I heard the answer, I said to myself, What can the god mean? and what is the interpretation of his riddle? for I know that I have no wisdom, small or great ...

After long perplexity, I thought of a method of trying the question. I reflected that if I could only find a man wiser than myself, then I might go to the god with a refutation in hand ... Accordingly I went to one who had the reputation of wisdom, and observed him – his name I need not mention, he was a politician; and in the process of examining him and talking with him, this, men of Athens, was what I found. I could not help thinking that he was not really wise, although he was thought wise by many, and still wiser by himself; and thereupon I tried to explain to him that he thought himself wise, but was not really wise; and the consequence was that he hated me, and his enmity was shared by several who were present and heard me. So I left him, saying to myself as I went away: Well, although I do not suppose that either of us knows anything really worth knowing, I am at least wiser than this fellow – for he knows nothing, and thinks that he knows; I neither know nor think that I know. In this one little point, then, I seem to have the advantage of him. Then I went to another who had still higher pretensions to wisdom, and my conclusion was exactly the same. Whereupon I made another enemy of him, and of many others besides him …

… the result of my mission was just this: I found that the men most in repute were nearly the most foolish; and that others less esteemed were really closer to wisdom … He, O men, is the wisest, who, like Socrates, knows that his wisdom is in truth worth nothing.

PLATO, *Apology*, from his account of Socrates' Apology before the court in Athens

W E THINK that knowledge and expertise belong rather to skill than to experience, and we assume that the skilled are wiser than the experienced, in that it is more in connection with knowledge that wisdom is associated with anything. And the reason for this is that the skilled know the cause, whereas the experienced do not. For the experienced know the 'that' but not the 'because', whereas the skilled have a grasp of the 'because', the cause.

That is why in each field designers are thought more prestigious and to have more knowledge than craftsmen and to be wiser, in that they know the causes for what is being done. The assumption is that it is not being practical that makes them wiser but their possession of an account and their grasp of the causes. And in general the ability to teach is a distinguishing mark between the knowledgeable and the ignorant man, and that is why we think that skill is rather a form of knowledge than experience. For the skilled can, whereas the merely experienced cannot, teach.

ARISTOTLE, *Metaphysics*, *Book Alpha*

Of the relation of soul and body

I F ... THERE is any of the functions or affections of the soul which is peculiar to it, it will be possible for it to be separated from the body. But if there is nothing peculiar to it, it will not be separable ...

It seems that all the affections of the soul involve the body – passion, gentleness, fear, pity, confidence, and further, joy and both loving and hating; for at the same time as these the body is affected in a certain way ...

If this is so, it is clear that the affections (of the soul) are principles involving matter. Hence their definitions are such as 'Being angry is a particular movement of a body of such and such a kind, or a part or potentiality of it, as a result of this thing and for the sake of that.' And for these reasons an inquiry concerning the soul ... is at once the province of the student of nature.

But the student of nature and the dialectician would define each of these differently, e.g. what anger is. For the latter would define it as a desire for retaliation or something of that sort, the former as the boiling of the blood and hot stuff round the heart. Of these, the one gives the matter, the other the

form and principle. For this is the principle of the thing, but it must be in a matter of such and such a kind if it is to be.

ARISTOTLE, *De Anima, Book 1*

WHEN YOU buy victuals and liquors you can carry them off from the dealer or merchant in separate vessels, and before you take them into your body by drinking or eating you can lay them by in your house and take the advice of an expert whom you can call in, as to what is fit to eat or drink and what is not, and how much you should take and when; so that in this purchase the risk is not serious. But you cannot carry away doctrines in a separate vessel: you are compelled, when you have handed over the price, to take the doctrine in your very soul by learning it, and so to depart either an injured or a benefited man.

PLATO, *Protagoras (314B)*

THE WISE can learn a great deal even from enemies. Take a proverb like 'Safety lies in circumspection.' You don't learn the truth of that from your friends, you learn it from your enemies, and pretty quickly too. It wasn't from their friends that cities learned to perfect their fortifications and build up their navies: it was from their enemies. Yet it's only through having learnt this lesson that they can protect their children, their homes and their property.

ARISTOPHANES, *The Birds*

On the impossibility of saying that nothing you say is true ...

FINALLY, IF nothing can be truly asserted, even the following claim would be false, the claim that there is no true assertion. And if there is a true assertion, this is a refutation of what is pretended by the raisers of these objections, being as they are the comprehensive eliminators of all debate.

ARISTOTLE, *Metaphysics*, *Book Kappa*

On Plato's notion of 'the Good'

THE HIGHEST object of knowledge is the essential nature of the Good, from which everything that is good and right derives its value for us ... without that knowledge, to 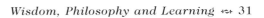 know everything else, however well, would be of no value to us, just as it is of no use to possess anything without getting the good of it. What advantage can there be in possessing everything except what is good, or in understanding everything else while of the good and desirable we know nothing? ... A thing, then, that every soul pursues as an end of all her actions, dimly divining its existence, but perplexed and unable to grasp its nature with the same clearness and assurance as in dealing with other things, and so missing whatever value those other things might have – a thing of such supreme importance is not a matter about which those chosen Guardians of the whole fortunes of our commonwealth can be left in the dark.

PLATO, *The Republic, Book XXIII*

THE
TALENTED

QUALITIES LIKE ready understanding, a good memory, sagacity, quickness, together with a high-spirited, generous temper, are seldom combined with willingness to live a quiet life of sober constancy. Keen wits are apt to lose all steadiness and to veer about in every direction. On the other hand, the steady reliable characters, whose impassivity is proof against the perils of war, are equally proof against instruction. Confronted with intellectual work, they become comatose and do nothing but yawn.

PLATO, *The Republic, Book XXIII*

FRIENDSHIP, LOVE AND PASSION

FRIENDSHIP

THE NOBLE man is chiefly concerned with wisdom and friendship; of these, the former is a mortal good, the latter an immortal.

EPICURUS

ONE PERSON wants to get possession of horses, another dogs, another money, and another distinctions: of these things I reckon little, but for the possession of friends I have quite a passionate longing ...

PLATO, *Lysis*

WHEN FRIENDS who have quarrelled come together,
Meet face to face, they have to think
Of only one thing – what they came for.
Nothing else. The past and past wrongs
Must have no place in their remembrance.

EURIPIDES, *The Phoenician Women*

NOBODY WOULD choose to live without friends even if he had all the other good things. Indeed those who hold wealth and office and power are thought to stand in special need of friends; for what is the use of such prosperity to them if they are denied the opportunity for beneficence, which is most commonly and most commendably directed towards friends? Or how can their prosperity be guarded and preserved without friends? because the greater it is, the more precarious. In poverty too and all the other misfortunes of life, people regard their friends as their only refuge.

ARISTOTLE, *Ethics, Book 8*

THOSE WHO are hasty in making friends are not to be approved; nor yet should you commend those who avoid friendship, for risks must be run for its sake.

EPICURUS

S O THOSE who love each other on the ground of utility do not love each other for their personal qualities, but only in so far as they derive some benefit from each other. Similarly with those who love one another on the ground of pleasure; because it is not for being a certain character that witty people are liked, but because we find them pleasant. So when people love one another on the ground of utility their affection is motivated by their own good, and when they love on the ground of pleasure it is motivated by their own pleasure; that is, they love the other person not for what he is, but *qua* useful or pleasant. So those friendships are accidental, because the person loved is not loved on the ground of his actual nature, but merely as providing some benefit or pleasure.

... Only the friendship of those who are good, and similar in their goodness, is perfect. For these people each alike wish good for the other *qua* good, and they are good in themselves. And it is those who desire the good of their friends for the friends' sake that are most truly friends, because each loves the other for what he is, and not for any incidental quality.

ARISTOTLE, *Ethics, Book 8*

FRIENDSHIP DANCES through the world, bidding us all to awaken and give thanks.

EPICURUS

A FEW friends for amusement are quite enough, like a pinch of seasoning in food ... So also there is a limit to the number of one's friends; and probably this would be the largest number with whom one can be on intimate terms – because this, as we saw, is the chief factor in friendship – and it is not hard to see that one cannot be intimate, and share oneself, with a large number of people. Besides, they too must be friends with one another if they are all to live as a group; and it is difficult to have this state of affairs when the numbers are large. It becomes difficult even to sympathise closely with the joys and sorrows of many, because one is likely to be faced with sharing the joy of one and the sorrow of another simultaneously. Probably, then, it is as well to aim at having not as many friends as possible, but only as many as are enough to form an intimate circle.

ARISTOTLE, Ethics, Book 9

HOSPITALITY

G REETINGS, STRANGER! Here in our house you'll find a royal welcome. Have supper first, then tell us what you need.'

HOMER, *The Odyssey*, *Book 1*

THIS STRANGER here, our guest –
I don't know who he is, or whether he comes
from sunrise lands or the western lands of evening,
but he has come in his wanderings to my palace:
he pleads for passage, he begs we guarantee it.
So now, as in years gone by, let us press on
and grant him escort. No one, I tell you, no one
who comes to *my* house will languish long here,
heartsick for home.

HOMER, *The Odyssey*, *Book 8*

LOVE

FOR THE guiding principle we should choose for all our days, if we are minded to live a comely life, cannot be acquired either by kinship or office or wealth or anything so well as by Love.

PLATO, *Symposium*, from the 'Speech of Phaedrus'

TRUE ENOUGH
Calypso the lustrous goddess tried to hold me back,
deep in her arching caverns, craving me for a husband.
So did Circe, holding me just as warmly in her halls,
the bewitching queen of Aeaea keen to have me too.
But they never won the heart inside me, never.
So nothing is as sweet as a man's own country,
his own parents, even though he's settled down
in some luxurious house, off in a foreign land
and far from those who bore him.

HOMER, *The Odyssey, Book 9*

THE MORE she spoke, the more a deep desire for tears
welled up inside his breast – he wept as he held the
    wife
he loved, the soul of loyalty, in his arms at last.
Joy, warm as the joy that shipwrecked sailors feel
when they catch sight of land – Poseidon has struck
their well-rigged ship on the open sea with gale winds
and crushing walls of waves, and only a few escape,
    swimming,
struggling out of the frothing surf to reach the shore,
their bodies crusted with salt but buoyed up with joy
as they plant their feet on solid ground again,
spared a deadly fate. So joyous now to her
the sight of her husband, vivid to her gaze,
that her white arms, embracing his neck
would never for a moment let him go.

HOMER, *The Odyssey*, *Book 23*

YOU ARE not speaking to a woman of no character,
nor to one who is ignorant of what human beings are like,
that they do not take pleasure in the same things for
    ever.
Whoever takes his stand in the ring against Love, gets

to grips with him like a boxer, undoubtedly has no sense.
Love rules over any of the gods he chooses, and
over me. So why not over other women like me?
If my husband has been caught by this sickness
<u>I should certainly be mad to find fault with him,</u>
or with this woman, who cannot be held responsible
for anything shameful, nor for any harm done to me.

SOPHOCLES, *Young Women of Trachis*

B UT IN emotional relations the lover sometimes complains
that his devotion is unrequited (it may be because he
has no loveable quality); and often the beloved
complains that the one who used to promise everything now
fulfils none of his promises. Such situations arise when the
one who loves his beloved on the ground of pleasure and the
other his lover on the ground of utility, and they no longer
possess these attributes; because a friendship based on these
motives breaks up as soon as the reasons for which the friends
loved each other no longer present themselves. For it was not
each other that they loved, but each other's <u>attributes</u>, which
were not permanent.

Love of attributes [handwritten marginal note]

ARISTOTLE, *Ethics, Book 8*

Friendship, Love and Passion ❧ 43

PASSION

THERE'S AN anger that goes beyond all remedy
When love turns to hate.

EURIPIDES, *Medea*

THE LOVER has a recollection of Beauty, but is parted from it and cannot comprehend it; he is overwhelmed by visible beauties as the present focus of his passion. He must be taught not to find rapture in the worship of a single body, but be guided by reason to see the same Beauty in all embodied forms, and be brought to understand its incorporeal nature and higher origin, and its truer manifestation in the immaterial. He should be shown the beauty in customs and laws, as a first lesson in disembodied loveliness, and learn to see the beauty in arts, science and virtues. Next, these forms of beauty must be brought under one principle, and their source explained. From virtues he must now ascend to Intellect, or Being itself; and once there, must tread the higher path.

PLOTINUS

PASSION. TOO much passion.
No merit in that,
No reputation there.
Love, gentle love,
Is a gift of the gods.
I'll settle for that,
With no searing, no poison,
No obsession, no pain.

Control. Moderation.
I'll pray for them,
I'll be comfortable with them.
God preserve me
From the madness,
The affliction that is sex,
Without rhyme, without reason.
Affection, but not passion.

EURIPIDES, *Medea*

I UNDERSTAND from you that your natural disposition is too much inclined toward sexual passion. Follow your inclinations as you will provided only that you neither violate the laws, disturb well-established customs, harm any one of your neighbours, injure your own body, nor waste your possessions. That you be not checked by some one of these provisions is impossible; for a man never gets any good from sexual passion, and he is fortunate if he does not receive harm.

EPICURUS

MARRIAGE

THE ROYAL couple, once they'd revelled in all
the longed-for joys of love, revelled in each other's
   stories,
the radiant woman telling of all she'd borne at home,
watching them there, the infernal crowd of suitors
slaughtering herds of cattle and good fat sheep –
while keen to win her hand –
draining the broached vats dry of vintage wine.
And great Odysseus told his wife of all the pains
he had dealt out to other men and all the hardships
he'd endured himself – his story first to last –
and she listened on, enchanted ...
Sleep never sealed her eyes till all was told.

HOMER, *The Odyssey, Book 23*

IN MAKING regulations about their partnerships he (the lawgiver) should have regard both for the spouses themselves and to their length of life, in order that they may arrive at the right ages together at the same time, so that the period of the father's ability to beget and that of the mother's to bear children may coincide. A period when one is capable and the other is not leads to mutual strife and quarrels.

... Accordingly we conclude that the appropriate age for the union is about the eighteenth year for girls and for men the thirty-seventh. With such timing, their union will take place when they are physically in their prime, and it will bring them down together at the end of procreation at exactly the right moment for both.

ARISTOTLE, *Politics, Book VII xvi*

AND MAY the gods give you all your heart desires:
husband and house, and lasting harmony too.
No finer, greater gift in the world than that ...
when man and woman possess their home, two minds,
two hearts that work as one. Despair to their enemies,
a joy to their friends. Their own best claim to glory.

HOMER, *The Odyssey, Book 6*

THE LOVE between husband and wife is considered to be naturally inherent in them. For man is by his nature a pairing rather than a social creature, inasmuch as the family is an older and more necessary thing than the state, and procreation is a characteristic more commonly shared with the animals. In the other animals partnership goes no further than this; but human beings cohabit not merely to produce children but to secure the necessities of life. From the outset the functions are divided, the husband's being different from the wife's; so they supply each other's deficiencies by pooling their personal resources. For this reason it is thought that both utility and pleasure have a place in conjugal love.

FAMILY PRECEDES STATE

ARISTOTLE *Ethics*, *Book 8*

THE STRONGEST fortress you can find,
A woman and a man in partnership.

EURIPIDES, *Medea*

MODERATION AND DILIGENCE

THE LUCKY man's great good fortune
Ruins his children.
This was old wisdom.
Is it true?
Surely the father who breaks heaven's law
Ruins his children.
The father who denies heaven's right
Blinds his children.
The father who forgets to be humble
Crushes his children.
Evil begets evil.
But the children of the man who fears heaven,
They tread with care. They care for the good.
They are rewarded.

Rich pride mounts rich pride
And begets insolence.
Pampered insolence begets
Anarchy.
And anarchy, where every man
Is the tyrant
Of his own conceit,
Begets all-out war –
Striking at heaven and earth.

ANARCHY

AESCHYLUS, *The Oresteia*

MODESTY AND SELF-RESTRAINT

IT IS not correct to speak of modesty as a kind of virtue, because it is more like a feeling than a state.... The feeling is not appropriate to every age: only to youth. We consider that adolescents ought to be modest because, living as they do under the sway of their feelings, they often make mistakes, but are restrained by modesty. Also we commend a modest youth, but nobody would comment an older man for being shamefaced, because we think that he ought not to do anything to be ashamed of.

ARISTOTLE, *Ethics, Book 4*

THE BRASH unbridled tongue,
The lawless folly of fools, will end in pain.
But the life of wise content
Is blest with quietness, escapes the storm
And keeps its house secure.
Though blessed gods dwell in the distant skies,
They watch the ways of men.
To know much is not to be wise.
Pride more than mortality hastens life to its end;
And they who in pride pretend

Beyond man's limits, will lose what lay
Close to their hand and sure.
I count it madness, and know no cure can mend
The evil man and his evil way.

EURIPIDES, *The Bacchae*

LIBERALITY IS recognised as such in relation to the giver's resources, because the liberality of an act depends not upon the number of the things given but upon the disposition of the giver and this makes him give according to his means. There is no reason why a man who gives less than another should not be more liberal, if his resources are smaller. People who have inherited their estate instead of acquiring it themselves are supposed to be more liberal, because they have not experienced shortage of money, and all people are fonder of what they have produced themselves – just like parents and poets.

ARISTOTLE, *Ethics, Book 4*

THE GREAT and exceptional thing perhaps belongs to others, to Socrates and his kind. 'Why, then, if we are endowed by nature for such greatness, do we not all achieve it?' Well, do all horses become fast? Are all dogs hunters? What then – if I lack talent, should I for that reason give up the effort? By no means. Epictetus will not be better than Socrates, but if I am no worse, that is enough for me. For I will not be Milo either, and nevertheless I do not neglect my body. Nor will I be Croesus, and nevertheless I don't neglect my possessions. In a word, we do not abandon any discipline out of despair of becoming the best.

EPICTETUS, *Discourses I*, chapter 2

ACCUSTOM YOURSELVES to eat barley cake and to drink water, and do not take fish and wine. For the latter, like the drugs of Circa, make old men bestial and young men effeminate.

CRATES *(a cynic)*

Excess

THE MAN who goes to <u>excess</u> and is <u>vulgar</u> exceeds ... by spending more than he ought. He uses trivial occasions to spend large sums of money and make a jarring display: e.g. by entertaining the members of his club as if they were wedding guests, and (if he is financing a comedy) by bringing on the chorus in purple robes at their first entrance, as they do at Megara. And all this he will do not from a fine motive but to show off his wealth, expecting to be admired for this sort of conduct; spending little where he ought to spend much, and much where he ought to spend little.

On the other hand the petty man will fall short in all respects. After spending vast sums he will spoil the beauty of the effect by some trifling detail; he hesitates over everything he does, considering how he can spend the least money, and lamenting over that, and assuming that he is doing everything on a larger scale than the occasion demands.

ARISTOTLE, *Ethics, Book 4*

I'M HARDLY a man for reckless, idle anger.
Balance is best in all things.

HOMER, *The Odyssey, Book 7*

SELF-SUFFICIENCY

(STOICISM)

WE REGARD self-sufficiency as a great good, not so that we may enjoy only a few things, but so that, if we do not have many, we may be satisfied with the few, being firmly persuaded that they take the greatest pleasure in luxury who regard it as least needed, and that everything that is natural is easily provided, while vain pleasures are hard to obtain. Indeed, simple sauces bring a pleasure equal to that of lavish banquets if once the pain due to need is removed; and bread and water give the greatest pleasure when one who is in need consumes them. To be accustomed to simple and plain living is conducive to health and makes a man ready for the necessary tasks of life. It also makes us more ready for the enjoyment of luxury if at intervals we chance to meet with it, and it renders us fearless against fortune.

EPICURUS, letter of Menoeceus

LET NOBODY tell you
Heaven ignores
The desecrator
Who mocks and defiles
The holy things –
For they are wrong.

Everywhere
The conceited man
With his lofty scheme
Ruins himself
And everybody near him.

The house where wealth
Cracks the foundations
With its sheer weight
Is a prison
Whose owner dies
In solitary.

What is enough?
Who knows? Once
A man in the stupor
Of wealth and pride
Has broken heaven's law
And kicked over
The altar of justice
It is too late.

Voluptuous promises,
Crystalline logic

2008 - 10 !

Caressing assurances
Lead him, the slave
Of his own destruction.

While guilt burns
Like a fixed star
The sleepless man
Feels his blood
And the light of his eye
Drained, and replaced
By a kind of filth.

Running after pleasure
Thoughtless, careless
As a boy
Chasing a bird.
He ruins his people.
He prays, but the gods
Are bedrock rock.
And men who pity him
Share his fate.

AESCHYLUS, *The Oresteia*

On moderating one's anger

IRASCIBLE PEOPLE get angry quickly and with the wrong people and at the wrong things and too violently, but they stop quickly, and this is the best thing about them. The reason for it is that they do not repress their anger but, being quick-tempered, vent it openly and then drop it.... Bitter people are hard to reconcile, and keep up their anger for a long time, because they suppress their animosity. Relief comes only with retaliation; for revenge provides release from anger by substituting pleasure for pain. In default of this they still labour under the weight of resentment; because owing to its concealment nobody helps to persuade the sufferer out of it, and it takes him time to digest his anger internally. People of this kind cause a great deal of trouble to themselves and their closest friends. We call people irritable if they get annoyed at the wrong things, and too much, and for too long a time, and if they are only pacified by inflicting vengeance or punishment.

ARISTOTLE, *Ethics*, *Book 4*

THE TEMPER of a tyrant
Can be a fearful thing.
A habit of power
Condones viciousness.
Better the quiet life.
I'll settle for mediocrity.
With peace of mind,
Moderation the watchword.
Ambition brings its own return,
God's envy. Further to fall.

EURIPIDES, *Medea*

ZEUS IS still great in heaven; he looks down
on everything, and has great power.
Yield your excessive anger up to him, do not
forget your enemies, nor hate them overmuch.

SOPHOCLES, *Electra*

Humour

BUFFOONS
V.
WITS

THOSE WHO go too far in being funny are regarded as buffoons and vulgar persons who exert themselves to be funny at all costs and who are more set upon raising a laugh than upon decency of expression and consideration for their victim's feelings. Those who both refuse to say anything funny themselves and take exception to the jokes of other people are regarded as boorish and sour; but those who exercise their humour with good taste are called witty, as one might say 'nimble witted'; because witticisms are considered to be movements of character, and characters, like bodies, are judged by their movements. As material for humour is ready to hand, and most people like fun and ridicule more than they should, even buffoons are called witty, as being good company; that there is a difference between the two, and not a small one, is clear from what we have said.

ARISTOTLE, *Ethics, Book 4*

PROGRESS IN THE VIRTUES

WHERE, THEN, is progress? If any of you renounces externals and turns his attention to his moral character, cultivating and perfecting it, so as to bring it in line with nature: elevated, free, unhindered, unimpeded, trustworthy and honourable; and has learned that whoever desires or avoids things not in his power can be neither faithful nor free, but must of necessity shift and fluctuate right along with them, and must subject himself to other people who can furnish or deprive him of these things; and if, again, from the time he gets up in the morning, he keeps and preserves these tenets, bathing as a faithful man, eating as an honourable man, in every situation equally practising his principles as the runner does when he applies the principles of running, or a singer those of musicianship. This, then, is the man who in truth is making progress, and has not left home in vain.

EPICTETUS, *Discourses I, chapter 4*

Body

TAKE CARE of your soul, but take care of the body only to the degree that necessity requires, and of externals not even that much. For happiness is not pleasure, on account of which we need externals, while virtue is complete without any externals.

CRATES *(a Cynic)*

Sport

COME, STRANGER, sir; won't you try your hand
at our contests now? If you have skill in any.
It's fit and proper for you to know your sports.
What greater glory attends a man, while he's alive,
than what he wins with his racing feet and striving
    hands:
Come and compete then, throw your cares to the
    wind!

HOMER, *The Odyssey, Book 8*

FOR BOTH excessive and insufficient exercise destroy one's strength, and both eating and drinking too much or too little destroy one's health, whereas the right quantity produces, increases and preserves it. So it is the same with temperance, courage and the other virtues. The man who shuns and fears everything and stands up to nothing becomes a coward; the man who is afraid of nothing at all, but marches up to every danger, becomes foolhardy. Similarly the man who indulges in every pleasure and refrains from none becomes licentious; but if a man behaves like a boor and turns his back on every pleasure, he is a case of insensibility. Thus temperance and courage are destroyed by excess and deficiency and preserved by the mean … *'THE MEAN'*

So with the virtues. It is by refraining from pleasures that we become temperate, and it is when we have become temperate that we are most able to abstain from pleasures. Similarly with courage; it is by habituating ourselves to make light of alarming situations and to face them that we become brave, and it is when we have become brave that we shall be most able to face an alarming situation.

ARISTOTLE, *Ethics, Book 2*

HE HAS become an old man on the day on which he forgot his past blessings.

EPICURUS

WE NEED courage and steadfastness for our work, philosophy for leisure, and restraint and a sense of justice in both contexts, but particularly at times of leisured peace. For war forces men to be just and restrained, but the enjoyment of prosperity, and leisure in peacetime, are apt rather to make them arrogant. Therefore a great sense of justice and much self-restraint are demanded of those who are thought to be successful and to enjoy everything the world regards as a blessing.

ARISTOTLE, *Politics, Book VII, xv*

WAR
+
PEACETIME
MORALITY

A FAMISHED fox, seeing some bunches of grapes hanging [from a vine which had grown] in a tree, wanted to take some, but could not reach them. So he went away saying to himself: 'Those are unripe.'

AESOP, *Fable 32*

SELF-ADORNMENT AND PHYSICAL BEAUTY

SELF-ADORNMENT personates gymnastic: with its rascally, deceitful, ignoble and illiberal nature it deceives men by forms and colours, polish and dress, so as to make them, in the effect of assuming an extraneous beauty, neglect the native sort that comes through gymnastic .... As self-adornment is to gymnastic, so is sophistry to legislation; and as cookery is to medicine, so is rhetoric to justice.

PLATO, *Gorgias (466)*

A HOUSE-FERRET, having fallen in love with a handsome young man, begged Aphrodite, goddess of love, to change her into a human girl. The goddess took pity on this passion and changed her into a gracious young girl. The young man, when he saw her, fell in love with her and led her to his home. As they rested in the nuptial chamber, Aphrodite, wanting to see if in changing body the house-ferret had also changed in character, released a mouse in the middle of the room. The house-ferret, forgetting her present condition, leapt up from the bed and chased the mouse in order to eat it. The indignant goddess changed her back to her former state.

AESOP, *Fable 76*

ONE MAN may fail to impress us with his looks
but a god can crown his words with beauty, charm,
and men look on with delight when he speaks out.
Never faltering, filled with winning self-control,
he shines forth at assembly grounds and people gaze
at him like a god when he walks through the streets.
Another man may look like a deathless one on high
but there's not a bit of grace to crown his words.

HOMER, *The Odyssey*, *Book 8*

A MASTER was in love with an ugly and ill-natured slave girl. With the money he gave her, she adorned herself with sparkling ornaments and rivalled her own mistress. She made continual sacrifices to Aphrodite, goddess of love, and beseeched her to make her beautiful. But Aphrodite appeared to the slave in a dream and said to her:

'I don't want to make you beautiful, because I am angry with this man for thinking that you already are.'

AESOP, *Fable 18*

On men remaining bearded!

IS THERE anything more <u>useful</u> than the hairs on the chin? But hasn't nature made use even of these in as becoming a manner as possible? Has it not through them distinguished the male from the female? Does not the nature of each one of us declare at once from afar, 'I am a man: on this basis approach me, on this basis talk to me. Look for nothing further, just consider the tokens.' Again, in the case of women, just as in their voice nature has mingled a softer note, so too it has removed the hair from their chins. But no, you say: 'The animal ought to have been left without distinguishing mark, and each of us should announce on his own account, "I am a man." But how fair and becoming and noble the token is! How much fairer than the cock's comb, how much more magnificent than the lion's mane! For this reason we ought to preserve the signs of god, we should not do away with them or, so far as in us lies, confuse the sexes that have been thus distinguished.

EPICTETUS, *Discourses I, chapter 16*

ON SEEKING WEALTH

NATURAL WEALTH is limited and easily obtained; the wealth defined by vain fancies is always beyond reach.

EPICURUS

YOU MAY tell me the pleasure of being rich outweighs everything. But to live surrounded by scandal, holding on to your money with both hands, beset by worry – has no appeal to me. A simple, untroubled life is what I want.

EURIPIDES, *Ion*

DO NOT spoil what you have by desiring what you have not; but remember that what you now have was once among the things only hoped for.

The wise man who has become accustomed to limited means knows better how to share with others than how to take from them, so great a treasure of self-sufficiency has he found.

EPICURUS

R EMEMBER, ALL success needs work.

SOPHOCLES, *Electra*

WEALTH FINDS me friends, and privileges,
and then finally the throne on high
of royal power, the nearest to the gods.
No one was ever born an enemy
to wealth – or if they are, they will not say.
For riches have a terrifying power to creep
in everywhere, even to sacred sites, and places where
a poor man, even if inside, could not obtain what he
    desires.
Wealth makes an ugly person beautiful,
an incoherent speaker clever with his tongue;
alone, wealth knows how to find joy even in
a sick-bed and conceals its miseries.

SOPHOCLES, *Aleus' Sons* (a fragment)

POWER & WEALTH

Knowing one's place

Atortoise begged an eagle to teach him to fly. The eagle pointed out that he was not made to fly – far from it! But the tortoise only pleaded with him even more. So the eagle took him in his talons, flew up into the air and then let him go. The tortoise fell on to the rocks and was smashed to pieces.

AESOP, *Fable 351*

COURAGE, FATE AND SUFFERING

COURAGE

FOR NOW there's War himself
marching against us – look!
parading before the walls.
Can you feel it, the lust for battle
rising …?
This is a time of blood and fire.
Oh save this city!
We cling together
one love one fear
one nation in mourning.
If this dear land of tall towers
should suffer –
one blood one race
descended all
from the horned moon-maiden Io,
we share one agony …

EURIPIDES, *The Phoenician Women*

I DO NOT describe animals, or anything else that from thoughtlessness has no fear of the dreadful, as courageous, but rather as fearless and foolish. Or do you suppose I describe all children as courageous, that have no fear because they are thoughtless? I rather hold that the fearless and the courageous are not the same thing. In my opinion very few people are endowed with courage and forethought, while rashness, boldness, and fearlessness, with no forethought to guide it, are found in a great number of men, women, children and animals. So you see, the acts that you and most people call courageous, I call rash, and it is the prudent acts which I speak of that are courageous.

FEARLESSNESS
v.
COURAGE.

PLATO, *Larches (197C)*

FATE

HE WAYS of the gods are involved and mysterious; they send us good and bad fortune in turn, and all is for the best. One man suffers, but soon his suffering is over and he prospers beyond his hopes; another man does not suffer, but when his turn comes the luck he enjoyed so long deserts him, and he perishes miserably. So you and your husband had your share of suffering – you were ill spoken of, he was caught in the storm of battle. As long as he struggled for what he wanted, he gained nothing; now good fortune has come to him of its own accord, and he's a happy man.

'ALL IS FOR THE BEST'
of LEIBNIZ
+ VOLTAIRE

EURIPIDES, *Helen*

WO COCKERELS were fighting over some hens. One triumphed and saw the other off. The defeated one then withdrew into a thicket where he hid himself. The victor fluttered up into the air and sat atop a high wall, where he began to crow with a loud voice. Straight away an eagle fell upon him and carried him off. And, from then on, the cockerel hidden in the shadows possessed all the hens at his leisure.

AESOP, *Fable 20*

POOR MAN, how much you've borne – pain to break the
   spirit!
What daring brought you down to the ships, all alone,
to face the glance of the man who killed your sons,
so many fine brave boys: You have a heart of iron.
Come, please, sit down on this chair here …
Let us put our griefs to rest in our own hearts,
rake them up no more, raw as we are with mourning.
What good's to be won from tears that chill the spirit:
So the immortals spun our lives that we, we wretched
   men
live on to bear such torments – the gods live free of
   sorrows.
There are two great jars that stand on the floor of
   Zeus's halls
and hold his gifts, our miseries one, the other blessings.
When Zeus who loves the lightning mixes gifts for a man,
now he meets with misfortune, now good times in turn.
When Zeus dispenses gifts from the jar of sorrows only,
he makes a man an outcast – brutal, ravenous hunger
drives him down the face of the shining earth,
stalking far and wide, cursed by gods and men.

HOMER, *The Iliad, Book 24*

O FATE, have you not from the beginning
Bred me wretched before all men,
Singled me out for suffering? My mother
Had not laboured yet to bring me to the light
Before Apollo told how I, unborn,
Should kill my father, and he, my begetter,
Knew me as his destined death, tried to destroy me,
Tore me from my mother's breast and threw me
To the mercy of wild beasts on the bleak
Mountain side. But I was saved.
Saved! O you place of desolation,
Why were you not sunk fathoms deep
In hell for not destroying me?
You let me go, let me be rescued,
Cared for at Polybus' court, lovingly
Led towards the horror of
My fate's fulfilment. I killed my father,
Bedded with my mother, got me her sons
Who were my brothers, and whom I now
Have killed, passing to them
The curse that Laius laid on me.
What does heaven want of me?
I was not born mad! Never could I
Have done such things of my own nature,

Courage, Fate and Suffering ↜ 87

Against my eyes, against my sons,
If the whole cruel senseless cycle
Had not been god-contrived against me!

EURIPIDES, *The Phoenician Women*, from the lament of Oedipus

OLYMPIAN ZEUS ordains,
The gods accomplish, strangely.
Things rarely end as you expect.
The unexpected is god's way,
The lesson of this story.

EURIPIDES, final lines of *Medea*

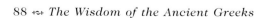

ΑΡΙΣΤΟΤΛΗΣ

Imago hæc Aristotelis Physicorum. Libros scribentis, pertinet ad I.

FACING DEATH

MY TIME has come:
At last the gods have called me down to death.
I thought he was at my side, the hero Deiphobus –
he's safe inside the walls, Athena's tricked me blind.
And now death, grim death is looming up beside me,
no longer far away. No way to escape it now. This,
this was their pleasure after all, sealed long ago –
Zeus and the son of Zeus, the distant deadly Archer –
though often before now they rushed to my defence.
So now I meet my doom. Well let me die –
but not without struggle, not without glory, no,
in some great clash of arms that even men to come
will hear of down the years!

HOMER, *The Iliad*, *Book 22*, the words of Hector

LET US reflect in another way, and we shall see that there
is great reason to hope that death is a good; for one of
two things – either death is a state of nothingness and
utter unconsciousness, or, as men say, there is a change and
migration of the soul from this world to another. Now if you
suppose that there is no consciousness, but a sleep like the

handwritten marginalia:
SOCRATES
1. NOTHINGNESS
or
2. MIGRATION
of
SOUL.

sleep of him who is undisturbed even by dreams, death will be an unspeakable gain. For if a person were to select the night in which his sleep was undisturbed even by dreams, and were to compare with this the other days and nights of his life, and then were to tell us how many days and nights he had passed in the course of his life better and more pleasantly than this one, I think that any man, I will not say a private man, but even the great king will not find many such days or nights, when compared with the others. Now if death be of such a nature, I say that to die is gain; for eternity is then only a single night. But if death is the journey to another place, and there, as men say, all the dead abide, what good, O my friends and judges, can be greater than this?

on possibility of afterlife

Wherefore, O judges, be of good cheer about death, and know of a certainty that no evil can happen to a good man, either in life or in death, and that he and his are not neglected by the gods …

The hour of departure has arrived, and we go our ways – I to die, and you to live. Which is better God only knows.

PLATO, *Apology* (of Socrates)

IRRELEVANCE

ACCUSTOM YOURSELF to the belief that death is of no concern to us, since all good and evil lie in sensation and sensation ends in death. Therefore the true belief that death is nothing to us makes a mortal life happy, not by adding to it an infinite time, but by taking away the desire for immortality. For there is no reason why the man who is thoroughly assured that there is nothing to fear in death should find anything to fear in life. So, too, he is foolish who says that he fears death, not because it will be painful when it comes, but because the anticipation of it is painful; for that which is no burden when it is present gives pain to no purpose when it is anticipated. Death, the most dreaded of evils, is therefore of no concern to us; for while we exist death is not present, and when death is present we no longer exist. It is therefore nothing either to the living or to the dead since it is not present to the living, and the dead no longer are.

'NOTHING'

EPICURUS, from a letter of Menoeceus

ON SUFFERING

AND I saw Tantalus too, bearing endless torture.
He stood erect in a pool, as the waters lapped his chin –
parched, he tried to drink, but he could not reach the
    surface,
no, time and again the old man stooped, craving a sip,
time and again the water vanished, swallowed down,
laying bare the caked black earth at his feet –
some spirit drank it dry. And over his head
leafy trees dangled their fruit from high aloft,
pomegranates and pears, and apples glowing red,
succulent figs and olives swelling sleek and dark,
but as soon as the old man would strain to clutch them
    fast
a gust would toss them up to the lowering clouds.
And I saw Sisyphus too, bound to his own torture,
grappling his monstrous boulder with both arms
    working,
heaving, hand struggling, legs driving, he kept on
thrusting the rock uphill towards the brink, but just
as it teetered, set to topple over –
                    time and again

the immense weight of the thing would wheel it back
and
the ruthless boulder would bound and tumble down to
the plain again –
so once again he would heave, would struggle to thrust
it up,
sweat drenching his body, dust swirling above his head.

HOMER, *The Odyssey, Book 11*

PEOPLE OF Thebes, look, this is Oidipous.
He knew the famous riddles. He was a mighty king.
He was the envy of everyone who saw how lucky he'd
been.
Now he's struck a wave of terrible ruin.
While you're alive, you must keep looking to
your final day, and don't be happy till
you pass life's boundary without suffering grief.

SOPHOCLES, final lines of *Oidipous [Oedipus]*

MEN HAVE no choice but to take whatever
is given them by the gods in the way of fortune.
But those who wrap themselves in misery by their own
    choice,
as is the case with you, have no right to receive
any sympathy or any pity from anyone at all.
You have become savage, and you accept no advice,
should someone who is well disposed to you offer it,
but hate the man, regarding him as an outright enemy.

SOPHOCLES, *Philoktetes*

LET ANY man whose life is pursued by misfortune reverence the gods and take courage. For in the end good men receive the reward they deserve; but evil natures beget evil fortune; and to them happiness can never come.

EURIPIDES, final lines of *Ion*

LEGITIMATE GRIEF

STRONG GRIEFS ask strong lamenting. Who shall be
Pattern and partner to my crying soul?
What tearful song can match the toll
Of deep pain paid by silent misery?

Come Seiran maidens, daughters of Earth,
Young and light of wing,
Come with Libyan flute, with pipe and string,
Bring music for my despair,
Share your tears to suit my sorrow,
Couple note with note, pain with my pain;
And when songs of death,
Solemn chants dear to departed souls,
Ring through the vaulted shades of death,
Hear and accept them, Queen Persephone,
Echoes of my heart's agony,
Offerings to fill my tears' deficiency.

EURIPIDES, *Helen*

TEKMESSA: ... NOW that he's sane again [of Aias] he has
    new suffering,
Looking at injuries you've caused yourself,   *SELF - DESTRUCTION*
when no one else contributed,
creates great suffering ...
Sailor: If he has stopped, I think all will be well;
the greater part of our torment is gone.
Tekmessa: If someone gave the choice, which would
    you take –
to hurt your friends, while you yourself were happy,
or be together with your friends and share their grief?
Sailor: Lady, a double suffering is worse.
Tekmessa: Then we're destroyed now his madness is gone.
Sailor: What do you mean? I do not understand.
Tekmessa: When he was mad, Aias himself found joy
in those perverted fantasies that bound him fast,
while he hurt us, who were sane, being here like that;
but he has been restored, and now, recovered from
    disease,
he's utterly prostrated by a dreadful grief
– and we are too, just as we were before.
Is this not double suffering instead of one?

SOPHOCLES, *Aias*

Courage, Fate and Suffering ❧ 99

IT'S SHAMEFUL for a man to want long life,
who sees unchanging misery.
Day follows day, pushing us on, pulling us back;
what joy is there, except in death?
I would not give the slightest value to someone
who warms his heart with empty hopes;
a man of noble birth must live a glorious life,
or die in glory. That is all.

SOPHOCLES, *Aias*

MORALITY

TEST EACH of your desires by this question: 'What will happen to me if that which this desire seeks is brought to fulfilment, and what if it is not?'

EPICURUS

IF THEN, our activities have some end which we want for its own sake, and for the sake of which we want all the other ends – if we do not choose everything for the sake of something else (for this will involve an infinite progression, so that our aim will be pointless and ineffectual) – it is clear that this must be the Good, that is the supreme good. Does it not follow, then, that a knowledge of the Good is of great importance to us for the conduct of our lives? Are we not more likely to achieve our aim if we have a target? If this is so, we must try to describe at least in outline what the Good really is, and by which of our sciences or faculties it is studied.

ARISTOTLE, *Ethics, Book 1:i*

SINCE ALL knowledge and every pursuit aims at some good, *of P*
what do we take to be the end of political science – what
is the highest of all practical goods? Well, so far as the
name goes there is pretty general agreement. 'It is happiness',
say both ordinary and cultured people; and they identify
happiness with living well and doing well. But when it comes
to saying in what happiness consists, opinions differ, and the
account given by the generality of mankind is not at all like
that of the wise. The former take it to be something obvious
and familiar, like pleasure or money or eminence, and there
are various other views; and often the same person actually
changes his opinion: when he falls ill he says that it is health,
and when he is hard up he says it is money.... Some, however,
have held the view that over and above these particular goods
there is another which is good in itself and the cause of *ABSOLUTE*
whatever goodness there is in all these others. *GOOD*

ARISTOTLE, *Ethics, Book 1:iv*

WE ALWAYS choose (happiness) for itself, and never for any other reason. It is different with honour, pleasure, intelligence and good qualities generally. We do choose them partly for themselves (because we should choose each one of them irrespective of any consequences); but we choose them also for the sake of our happiness, in the belief that they will be instrumental in promoting it. On the other hand nobody chooses happiness for *their* sake, or in general for any other reason.

ARISTOTLE, *Ethics, Book 1:vii*

PENTHEUS, PAY heed to my words. You rely
On force; but it is not force that governs human affairs.
Do not mistake for wisdom that opinion which
May rise from a sick mind. Welcome this god
    (Dionysius) to Thebes,
Offer libations to him, celebrate his rites.
Put on his garland. Dionysius will not compel
Women to be chaste, since in all matters self-control
Resides in our own natures. You should consider this;
For in the Bacchic ritual, as elsewhere, a woman
Will be safe from corruption if her mind is chaste.

EURIPIDES, *The Bacchae*

THE PHILOSOPHER has notions of good and evil unlike those of other men. For they are courageous because they are afraid of greater dangers, and temperate because they desire greater pleasures. But he disdains this balancing of pleasures and pains, which is the exchange of commerce and not of virtue. All the virtues, including wisdom, are regarded by him only as purifications of the soul.

PLATO, *Phaedo*

SOCIETY

IT IS not the country that makes good men, nor the city bad ones, but rather the time spent with good men and bad. Consequently, if you want your sons to become good men and not bad, send them, not to the country, but to a philosopher's school, where we, too, went and learned the fine things of life. For virtue is something acquired by practice and does not spontaneously enter the soul as evil does.

CRATES (a Cynic)

YOU MUST consider that of the desires some are natural, some are vain, and of those that are natural, some are necessary, others only natural. Of the necessary desires, some are necessary for happiness, some for the ease of the body, some for life itself. The man who has a perfect knowledge of this will know how to make his every choice or rejection tend toward gaining health of body and peace (of mind), since this is the final end of the blessed life. For to gain this end, namely freedom from pain and fear, we do everything. When once this condition is reached, all the storm of the soul is stilled, since the creature need make no move in search of anything that is lacking, nor seek after anything else to make complete the welfare of the soul and the body. For we only feel the lack of pleasure when from its absence we suffer pain; but when we do not suffer pain, we no longer are in need of pleasure. For this reason we say that pleasure is the beginning and the end of the blessed life. We recognise pleasure as the first and natural good; starting from pleasure we accept or reject; and we return to this as we judge every good thing, trusting this feeling of pleasure as our guide....

Handwritten margin notes: EVERY CHOICE / END: HEALTH of BODY + PEACE of MIND / PLEASURE - A GUIDE

For the very reason that pleasure is the chief and the natural good, we do not choose every pleasure, but there are times when we pass by pleasures if they are outweighed by the hardships that follow; and many pains we think better than pleasures when a greater pleasure will come to us once we have undergone the long-continued pains.

EPICURUS, letter to Menoeceus

BUT AMONG the many statements we have made, while all the rest are refuted this one alone is unshaken – that doing wrong is to be more carefully shunned than suffering it; that above all things a man should study not to seem but to be good both in private and in public; that if one becomes bad in any respect one must be corrected; that this is good in the second place – next to being just, to become so and to be corrected by paying the penalty; and that every kind of flattery, with regard either to oneself or to others, to few or to many, must be avoided; and that rhetoric is to be used for this one purpose always, of pointing to what is just, and so is every other activity.

PLATO, *Gorgias (527D)*

MORAL GOODNESS ... is the result of habit, from which it has got its name, being a slight modification of the word *ethos*. This fact makes it obvious that none of the moral virtues is engendered in us by nature, since nothing that is what it is by nature can be made to behave differently by habituation ... The moral virtues, then, are engendered in us neither *by* nor *contrary to* nature; we are constituted by nature to receive them, but their full development in us is due to habit....

But the virtues we do acquire by first exercising them, just as happens in the arts. Anything that we have to learn to do we learn by the actual doing of it: people become builders by building and instrumentalists by playing instruments. Similarly we become just by performing just acts, temperate by temperate ones, brave by performing brave ones ... In a word, then, like activities produce like dispositions. Hence we must give our activities a certain quality, because it is their characteristics that determined the resulting dispositions. So it is a matter of no little importance what sort of habits we form from the earliest age – it makes a vast difference, or rather all the difference in the world.

ARISTOTLE, *Ethics, Book 2*

ODYSSEUS: I am instructing you to take Philoktetes by a trick.

Neoptolemos: Why should we take him by a trick, rather than by persuasion?

Odysseus: He will not be persuaded, and you won't take him by force.

Neoptolemos: Are his strength and his determination that terrible?

Odysseus: His arrows are inescapable, and they deal out death.

Neoptolemos: So much so that no one would dare to confront him?

Odysseus: No, unless he is taken by trickery, as I say.

Neoptolemos: Do you not think it is shameful to tell lies?

Odysseus: No, not if telling lies brings you security.

Neoptolemos: So how does one find the face to mouth them?

Odysseus: You don't hold back, if you stand to gain.

SOPHOCLES, *Philoktetes*

So VIRTUE is a purposive disposition, lying in a mean that is relative to us and determined by a rational principle, and by that which a prudent man would use to determine it. It is a mean because two kinds of vice, one of excess and the other of deficiency; and also for this reason, that whereas these vices fall short of or exceed the right measure in both feelings and actions, virtue discovers the mean and chooses it … but not every action or feeling admits to a mean; because some have names that directly connote depravity, such as malice, shamelessness and envy, and among actions adultery, theft and murder. All these, and more like them, are so called as being evil in themselves; it is not the excess or deficiency of them that is evil. In their case, then, it is impossible to act rightly; one is always wrong. Nor does acting rightly or wrongly in such cases depend upon circumstances – whether a man commits adultery with the right woman or at the right time or in the right way, because to do anything of that kind is simply wrong.

ARISTOTLE, *Ethics, Book 2*

MORALITY AND THE GODS

YOU FEAR the gods so don't, on any account,
make light of them. Be firm in your belief
that they see when mortals do what's right,
and when they do what's wrong. The unholy
have never yet found an escape.

SOPHOCLES, *Oidipous at Kolonos*

I MUST REMONSTRATE with Apollo: what can have come over
him? He ravishes girls by force, then abandons them? He
begets children by stealth, then leaves them to die? Apollo,
no! Since you possess power, pursue goodness! Why, if a man
is bad, it is the gods who punish him. How can it be right for
you to make laws for men, and appear as lawbreakers
yourselves? ... It is unjust to call men bad for copying what
the gods find good: the sin lies with our examples!

EURIPIDES, *Ion*

THE LIST of murder, marriage, accidents
you rattle off so readily, I unfortunately had
to bear against my will. But it suited the gods.
Perhaps they've always had a grudge against our
    household.
But you'd not find a thing to blame me for –
on my own – that led me to commit
those wrongs against my family and myself.
    …
But I won't be condemned because I married
thus or killed my father – which you always
throw up in my face in bitter reproach.
Answer me this one question I put to you:
if someone tried to kill you – and you were innocent –
here on the spot, you ask if he was
your father or immediately fight back?
You'd fight back, I expect, if you loved
life, not look around to see what's right.
I walked into these misfortunes trapped
by the gods. And I believe my father,
were he still alive, would not deny me.

SOPHOCLES, *Oidipous at Kolonos*

MAN CANNOT do good
Without fear of the consequences
Of doing evil.
If the work of man's hand
Is not supervised by the Furies
That hand will stop at nothing.
The man without fear of the law
Will easily kill, as if by nature.
And the city without fear of the law
Is that killer's playground.

Lawless freedom is evil.
The tyrant's penal code is evil.
Freedom in one pan of the balance,
Stern rule in the other –
Where these stand in equilibrium
The scales are in the hand of God.
An evil heart
Has an evil hand.
A good heart has a hand
Blessed and able to bless.

AESCHYLUS, *The Oresteia*

MORALITY AND THE APPETITES

CHILDREN ... LIVE as their desires impel them, and it is in them that the appetite for pleasant things is strongest; so unless it is rendered docile and submissive to authority it will pass all bounds. For the irrational being the appetite for what gives it pleasure is insatiable and indiscriminate, and the exercise of the desire increases its innate tendency; and if these appetites are strong and violent, they actually drive out reason. So they must be moderate and few, and in no way opposed to the dictates of principle – this is what we mean by 'docile' and 'restrained' – and just as the child ought to live in accordance with the directions of his tutor, so the desiderative element in us ought to be controlled by the rational principle.

ARISTOTLE, *Ethics, Book 3*

CHILDREN

IRRATIONAL

MODERATION

(MATERIAL)
ATTACHMENTS

B UT ALTHOUGH we can care for, and attach ourselves to, one thing only, we choose instead to care for and attach ourselves to many things: the body, possessions, brother, friend, child, slave. And being tied to many things, we are weighed down and dragged along with them. And so, if the weather forbids us to sail, we sit down and fidget and keep peering about. 'What wind is blowing?' 'The north wind.' 'What good is that to us? When will the west wind blow?' 'When it wants to, or when it pleased Aeolus.' 'What then must we do?' 'Make the best of what is in our power, and use the rest according to its nature.' 'And what is its nature?' 'However god wishes it.'

[FATALISM]

EPICTETUS, *Discourses I*, chapter 1

A UTILITARIAN APPROACH AND
PURSUIT OF THE GOOD

WHAT UNWORTHINESS can there be in pleasure as against pain, save an excess or defect of one compared with the other? That is, when one becomes greater and the other smaller, or when there are more on one side and fewer on the other, or here a greater degree and there a less. For if you should say: But, Socrates, the immediately pleasant differs widely from the subsequently pleasant or painful, I should reply: Do they differ in anything but pleasure and pain? That is the only distinction. Like a practised weigher, put pleasant things and painful in the scales, and with them the nearness and the remoteness, and tell me which count for more. For if you weigh pleasant things against pleasant, the greater and the more are always preferred: if painful against painful, then always the fewer and smaller. If you weigh pleasant against painful, and find that the painful are out-balanced by the pleasant – whether the near by the remote or the remote by the near – you must take that course of action to which the pleasant are attached; but not that course if the pleasant are outweighed by the painful....

Well then, my friends, since we have found that the salvation of our life depends on making a right choice of pleasure and pain – of the more and the fewer, the greater and

PLEASURE
v.
PAIN

'WEIGH'
[SELF-
ANALYSIS]

the smaller, and the nearer and the remoter – is it not evident, in the first place, that measurement is a study of their excess and defect and equality in relation to one another? ...

Then if ... the pleasant is good, no one who has knowledge or thought of other actions as better than those he is doing, and as possible, will do as he proposes if he is free to do the better ones; and this yielding to oneself is nothing but ignorance, and mastery of oneself is as certainly wisdom.

SELF-MASTERY

They all agreed.

Well then, by ignorance do you mean having a false opinion and being deceived about matters of importance?

They all agreed to this also.

Then surely, I went on, no one willingly goes after evil or what he thinks to be evil; it is not in human nature, apparently, to do so – to wish to go after what one thinks to be evil in preference to the good; and when compelled to choose one of two evils, nobody will choose the greater when he may choose the lesser.

NO ONE WILLS EVIL [SELF-INTEREST]

PLATO, *Protagoras (358)*

AMBITION
Is the very soul of wrong. It enters in
Where there is harmony and happiness
And tears them apart, this spirit that drives you.
Others have rights too. Respect them. It were better
Far to do so. How is friend ever bound
To friend, city to city or ally to ally
Except as equals? How but as equals
Can men share this world as nature intended?
To have or have not, to be greater or less –
Each is foe to the other. Set them up
And the days of hate dawn.
Do we not weigh, measure, number our lives
By due proportion, by allotted share?
Does not the night's dark eye divide with day
An equal pacing of their yearly round
Without resentment that each gives place to other?
They serve their turn humbly, night and day.

EURIPIDES, *The Phoenician Women*

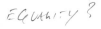
EQUALITY?

THE ROLES OF MEN AND WOMEN

YOU YOURSELVES, at the very outset of founding our commonwealth, agreed that everyone should do the one work for which nature fits him ... and isn't there a very great difference in nature between man and woman? ... Does not that natural difference imply a corresponding difference in the work to be given to each? ... That is why I shrank from touching upon these laws concerning the possession of wives and the rearing of children.

PLATO, *The Republic*, Book XI

DEFINITIONS OF GOOD

LET US now turn back again to the good, which is the object of our search, and ask what it can possibly be; because it seems to vary with the action or art. It is one thing in medicine and another in strategy, and similarly in all the other sciences. What, then, is the good of each particular one? Surely it is that for the sake of which everything else is done. In medicine, it is health; in strategy, victory; in architecture, a building – different things in different arts, but in every action and pursuit it is the *end*, since it is for the sake of this that everything else is done....

So, if there is only one final end, this will be the good of which we are in search; and if there are more than one, it will be the most final of these ...

Now we call an object pursued for its own sake more final than one pursued because of something else ... and that which is always choosable for its own sake and never because of something else we call final without any qualification.

ARISTOTLE, *Ethics*

BEAUTY, ART AND HAPPINESS

BEAUTY

AND CATCHING sight of Helen moving along the ramparts,
    they murmured one to another, gentle, winged
    words:
'Who on earth could blame them? Ah, no wonder the
    men of Troy and Argives under arms have suffered
    years of agony all for her, for such a woman.
Beauty, terrible beauty!
A deathless goddess – so she strikes the eyes!
            But still
ravishing as she is, let her go home in the long ships
and not be left behind ... for us and our children
down the years an irresistible sorrow.'

HOMER, *The Iliad*, *Book 3*

BEGINNING FROM obvious beauties he must for the sake of that highest beauty be ever climbing aloft, as on the rungs of a ladder, from one to two, and from two to all beautiful bodies; from personal beauty he proceeds to beautiful observances, from observances to beautiful learning, and from learning at last to that particular study which is concerned with the beautiful itself and that alone; so that in the end he comes to know the very essence of beauty.

PLATO, *Symposium (212)*

ART AND POETRY

I REFUSE TO give the name of art to anything that is irrational.

PLATO, *Gorgias (465C)*

AND WHAT does the inner sight behold? At its first awakening it cannot bear the brightness of the vision. So the soul itself must be trained, first to behold beautiful customs, then works of beauty – not those produced by the arts, but by the virtue of men of good repute – and next, observe the souls of those who fashion these beauties.

How might you see the beauty of a virtuous soul? Retire into yourself, and look; and if you cannot yet see beauty in yourself, learn from the sculptor giving beauty to his statue: he cuts away here and polishes there, smoothing and cleaning, till his statue wears a beautiful face. You similarly, must cut away excesses, straighten what is crooked, lighten what is dark and make it bright, and never cease from 'working on your statue' till the godlike glory of virtue shines out on you, till you see 'righteousness firmly established on its holy pedestal.'

PLOTINUS

EXCELLENCE OF form and content in discourse and of musical expression and rhythm, and grace and form and movement, all depend on goodness of nature, by which I mean, not the foolish simplicity sometimes called by courtesy 'good nature', but a nature in which goodness of character has been well and truly established....

So, if our young men are to do their proper work in life, they must follow after these qualities wherever they may be found. And they are to be found in every sort of workmanship, such as painting, weaving, embroidery, architecture, the making of furniture; and also in the human frame and in all the works of nature: in all these grace and seemliness may be present or absent. And the absence of grace, rhythm, harmony is nearly allied to baseness of thought and expression and baseness of character; whereas their presence goes with that moral excellence and self-mastery of which they are the embodiment....

Then we must compel our poets, on pain of expulsion, to make their poetry the express image of noble character; we must also supervise craftsmen of every kind and forbid them to leave the stamp of baseness, licence, meanness, unseemliness, on painting and sculpture, or building, or any other work on their hands; and anyone who cannot obey shall not practise his art in our commonwealth.

PLATO, *Republic, chapter IX*

IT IS clear that the poet's job is not to tell what has happened but the kind of things that can happen ... the difference between the historian and the poet is not in their presenting accounts that are versified or not versified, since it would be possible for Herodotus' work to be put into verses and it would be no less a kind of history with verse than it is without verses; rather the difference is this: the one tells us what has happened, the other the kind of things that can happen. And in fact that is why the writing of poetry is a more philosophical activity, and one to be taken more seriously, than the writing of history; for poetry tells us rather the universals, history the particulars.

ARISTOTLE, *Poetics, chapter 9*

Beauty, Art and Happiness ❧ 131

IF HOMER had really possessed the knowledge qualifying him to educate people and make them better men, instead of merely giving us a poetical representation of such matters, would he not have attracted a host of disciples to love and revere him? …

Can we suppose that Homer's contemporaries, or Hesiod's, would have left them to wander about reciting their poems, if they had really been capable of helping their hearers to be better men?

We conclude, then, that all poetry, from Homer onwards, consists in representing a semblance of its subjects, whatever it may be, including any kind of human excellence, with no grasp of the reality … the poet, knowing nothing more than how to represent appearances, can paint in words his picture of any craftsman so as to impress an audience which is equally ignorant and judges only by the form of expression; the inherent charm of metre, rhythm, and musical setting is enough to make them think that he has discoursed admirably about generalship or shoemaking or any other technical subject. Strip what the poet has to say of its poetical colouring, and I think you must have seen what it comes to in plain prose. It is like a face which was never really handsome, when it has lost the fresh bloom of youth.

PLATO, *The Republic, chapter XXXV*

DRAMATIC POETRY has a most formidable power of corrupting even men of high character, with a few exceptions …

Let me put the case for you to judge. When we listen to some hero of Homer or on the tragic stage moaning over his sorrows in a long tirade, or to a chorus beating their breasts as they chant a lament, you know how the best of us enjoy giving ourselves up to follow the performance with eager sympathy. The more a poet can move our feelings in this way, the better we think him. And yet when the sorrow is our own, we pride ourselves on being able to bear it quietly like a man, condemning the behaviour we admired in the theatre as womanish. Can it be right that the spectacle of a man behaving as one would scorn and blush to behave oneself should be admired and enjoyed, instead of filling us with disgust?

DANGER of SELF-PITY

… Few, I believe, are capable of reflecting that to enter into another's feelings must have an effect on our own: the emotions of pity our sympathy has strengthened will not be easy to restrain when we are suffering ourselves.

PLATO, *The Republic, Book XXXVII*

THE GIFT which you possess of speaking excellently about Homer is not an art but ... an inspiration; there is a divinity moving you, like that contained in the stone which Euripides calls a magnet, but which is commonly known as the stone of Heracles. This stone not only attracts iron rings, but also imparts to them a similar power of attracting other rings; and sometimes you may see a number of pieces of iron and rings suspended from one another so as to form quite a long chain: and all of them derive their power of suspension from the original stone. In like manner the Muse first of all inspires men herself; and from these inspired persons a chain of other persons is suspended, who take the inspiration. For all good poets, epic as well as lyric, compose their beautiful poems not by art, but because they are inspired and possessed. And as the Corybantian revellers when they dance are not in their right mind, so the lyric poets are not in their right mind when they are composing their beautiful strains: but when falling under the power of music and metre they are inspired and possessed; like Bacchic maidens who

INSPIRATION

(POST-MODERN!)

draw milk and honey from the rivers when they are under the influence of Dionysius but not when they are in their right mind. And the soul of the lyric poet does the same, as they themselves say; for they tell us that they bring songs from honeyed fountains, culling them out of the gardens and dells of the Muses; they, like the bees, winging their way from flower to flower. And this is true. For the poet is a light and winged and holy thing, and there is no invention in him until he has been inspired and is out of his senses, and reason is no longer in him: no man, while he retains that faculty, has the oracular gift of poetry.

PLATO, Ion

THE POET
'Holy'

On literature, education and censorship

IT SEEMS, then, our first business will be to supervise the making of fables and legends, rejecting all which are unsatisfactory; and we shall induce nurses and mothers to tell their children only those which we have approved, and to think more of moulding their souls through these stories than they now do of rubbing their limbs to make them strong and shapely. Most of the stories now in use must be discarded ...

We shall not tell a child that, if he commits the foulest crimes or goes to any length in punishing his father's misdeeds, he will be doing nothing out of the way, but only what the first and greatest of the gods have done before him ... Nor yet any tales of warfare and intrigues and battles of gods against gods, which are equally untrue ... If by any means we can make (the future Guardians) believe that no one has ever had a quarrel with a fellow citizen and it is a sin to have one, that is the sort of thing our old men and women should tell children from the first; and as they grow older, we must make the poets write for them in the same strain. Stories like those of Hera being bound by her son, or of Hephaestus flung from heaven by his father for taking his mother's part when she was beaten, and all those battles of the gods in Homer, must not be admitted into our state, whether they be allegorical or not ...

Next, our young men will need self-control; and for the mass of mankind that chiefly means obeying their governors, and themselves governing their appetite for the pleasures of eating and drinking and sex. Here again we shall disapprove of much that we find in Homer.

PLATO, *The Republic, Book IX*

HAPPINESS AND TAKING PLEASURE

WE ARE now in a position to define the happy man as 'one who is <u>active in relation to complete virtue</u>, and who are <u>adequately furnished with external goods</u>, and that not for some unspecified period but throughout a complete life.'

DEFINITION
I VIRTUE
II MATERIAL GOODS (PROPERTY)

ARISTOTLE, *Ethics, Book 1*

DIONYSIUS, SON of Zeus, delights in banquets;
And his dear love is <u>Peace</u>, giver of wealth,
Saviour of young men's lives – a goddess rare!
In wine, his gift that charms all griefs away,
Alike both rich and poor may have their part.
His enemy is the man who has no care
To pass his years in happiness and health,
His days in quiet and his nights in joy.
Watchful to keep <u>aloof</u> both mind and heart
From men whose <u>pride</u> claims more than mortals may.

DIONYSIUS

DANGER OF PURSUIT OF VIRTUE → ARROGANCE + PRIDE

EURIPIDES, *The Bacchae*

WE MUST first distinguish pleasures of the soul from pleasures of the body. Examples of the former are love of civic distinction and love of learning. In either case when the subject enjoys what he loves it is not his body that is affected but rather his _mind_; and those who are concerned with pleasures of this sort are called neither temperate nor licentious. Similarly with all the others who are concerned with pleasures that are not physical. Those who like to hear marvellous tales or to relate anecdotes or to spend their days in aimless gossip we call idle and talkative, but not licentious; nor should we so describe those who are grieved at the loss of money or friends.

It is the pleasures of the body, then, that are the concern of _temperance_; but not even all of these. Those who enjoy the objects of sight, like colours and shapes and pictures, are called neither temperate nor licentious. It may be supposed, however, that even in the case of these pleasure can be felt in the right degree, or too much, or too little. Similarly with the objects of hearing. Nobody calls people licentious for taking an inordinate pleasure in listening to music or an actor's voice, nor temperate if their enjoyment was duly restrained. Nor do we speak in this way about those who enjoy smells, except those who do so by association. We do not call those who enjoy the smell of apples or roses or incense licentious.

ARISTOTLE, *Ethics, Book 3*

THE ARGUMENT that pleasures are bad because some pleasant things are injurious to health, is the same as saying that healthful things are bad because some healthful things are bad for the pocket. Both are bad in this limited sense, but that does not prove them to be bad in themselves, since even contemplation is sometimes injurious to health.

ARISTOTLE, *Ethics, Book 7*

TO SPEND effort and toil for the sake of amusement seems silly and unduly childish; but on the other hand the maxim of Anacharsis, 'Play to work harder', seems to be on the right lines, because amusement is a form of relaxation, and people need relaxation because they cannot exert themselves continuously.

ARISTOTLE, *Ethics, Book 10*

ONE MAY suppose that everyone feels drawn towards pleasure, because everyone is eager to live. Life is a form of activity, and each individual directs his activity to those objects, and by means of those faculties, that he likes best: e.g. the musician occupies himself with the sounds of music by the use of his hearing, and the student with the objects of study by the use of his intellect, and similarly with all the other examples. The pleasure perfects the activities, and so perfects life, to which all are drawn. It is quite reasonable, then, that they should also be eager for pleasure; because it perfects life for each individual, and life is the thing to choose. Whether we choose life on account of pleasure or pleasure on account of life is a question that may be dismissed at the moment; for it appears that they are closely connected and do not admit of separation: as pleasure does not occur without activity, so every activity is perfected by its pleasure.

ARISTOTLE, *Ethics, Book 10*

JUSTICE AND POLITICS

TRUTH IS so simple. A just cause
Needs no devious defence. It argues
Its own rightness. It is the wrong
Which is so sickly weak it can't stand up
Without the help of dubious doctoring.

EURIPIDES, *The Phoenician Women*

IF A MAN is cruel by nature, cruel in action,
the mortal world will call down curses on his head
while he is alive, and all will mock his memory after
  death.
But if a man is kind by nature, kind in action,
his guests will carry his fame across the earth
and people all will praise him from the heart.

HOMER, *The Odyssey, Book 19*

NO MAN can be a winner on this earth
Without being cursed by the envy of the rest.
The courage to win is the courage to face envy.

AESCHYLUS, *The Oresteia*

Natural justice is a compact resulting from expediency by which men seek to prevent one man from injuring others and to protect him from being injured by them. There is no such thing as justice or injustice among those beasts that cannot make agreements not to injure or be injured. This is also true of those tribes that are unable or unwilling to make agreements not to injure or be injured.

handwritten margin note: NATURAL JUSTICE.

handwritten margin note: BARBARIANS

EPICURUS

A MAN of lower rank shows that his character is bad
if he does not obey the people who're in power.
Law and good order cannot prosper in a city where
there is no element of fear;
nor can an army have the proper discipline
if there is not the barrier of fear and of respect.
Even a man of great physique should realise
that something small can bring him down.
If someone has both fear and deference,
be sure that they will keep him safe;
but where there's licence to be violent and do
just anything you want, know such a city will some
    time
lose favourable winds, and sink into the depths.

handwritten margin note: NECESSITY of FEAR + DEFERENCE

No! Let me see fear put in place where it's appropriate;
and let's not think that if we do all we desire
we will not pay the price of suffering.

SOPHOCLES, *Aias*

REVENGE BEGETS revenge,
Truth spins and evaporates
As blood drains from the head.
It is the law of Zeus:
A life for a life.
What is a human life worth?
More than itself, more than a life,
Or less? Or precisely the same?
The law of Zeus demands
A life for a life.
All – for all.
But this law of Zeus
Is a kind of disease
Inherited through the blood.
See how it has crazed
Every member of this house.

AESCHYLUS, *The Oresteia*

Justice

JUSTICE LIVES in poverty.
She survives. She measures
What is necessary.
She honours what ought to be honoured.
She seeks out clean hearts, clean hands.
She knows what wealth and power
Grind to dust between them. She knows
Goodness and the laws of heaven.

AESCHYLUS, *The Oresteia*

On rulers

THE BIRDS were consulting together on the choice of a king. The peacock demanded to be named king by virtue of his beauty. And the birds were about to vote for him when the jackdaw called out: 'But if you reign, what help can we expect from you when the eagle comes hunting for us?'

AESOP, *Fable 334*

Futility of war

WHAT LASTING thanks in the long run
for warring with our enemies, on and on, no end?
One and the same lot for the man who hangs back
and the man who battled hard. The same honour waits
for the coward and the brave. They both go down to
    Death,
the fighter who shirks, the one who works to
    exhaustion.
And what's laid up for me, what pittance? Nothing –
and after suffering hardships, year in, year out,
staking my life on the mortal risks of war.

HOMER, *The Iliad*, Book 9

On the origins of justice and politics

MAN SOON was enabled by his skill to articulate speech and words, and to invent dwellings, clothes, sandals, beds, and the foods that are of the earth. Thus far provided, men dwelt separately from the beginning, and cities there were none; so that they were being destroyed by the wild beasts, since these were in all ways stronger than they; and although their skill in handiwork was a sufficient aid in respect of food, in their warfare with the beasts it was defective; for as yet they had no civic art, which includes the art of war. So they sought to band themselves together and secure their lives by founding cities. Now as often as they were banded together they did wrong to one another through the lack of civic art, and thus they began to be scattered again and to perish. So Zeus, fearing that our race was in danger of utter destruction, sent Hermes to bring respect and right among men, to the end that there should be regulation of cities and friendly ties to draw them together. Then Hermes asked Zeus in what manner then was he to give men right and respect: 'Am I to deal them out as the arts have been dealt? That dealing was done in such wise that one man possessing medical art is able to treat many ordinary men, and so with the other craftsmen. Am I to place among men right and respect in this same way also ... or deal them out to all?' 'To all,' replied Zeus; 'let all have their share; for the cities cannot be formed if only a few have a share of these as of other arts. And make thereto a law of my ordaining, that he who cannot partake of respect and right shall die the death as a public pest.'

PLATO, *Protagoras (322)*

152 ❧ *The Wisdom of the Ancient Greeks*

JUSTICE BRINGS everything to a balance.
For every word a word, for hatred hatred,
For every fatal stroke a fatal stroke,
For sacrilege a violent death.
For pride – the neck broken.
Three generations of suffering
Have tested the truth of this law.

AESCHYLUS, *The Oresteia*

JUSTICE IS the anvil where Fate
Forges the blade.
Murder begets murder.
A life must pay for a life.
The avenger,
The demon of patience and cunning,
Waits for the moment,
Then demands the full price.

AESCHYLUS, *The Oresteia*

LAW IS a good thing, but it is not superior to philosophy. For the former compels a man not to do wrong, but the latter teaches him not to do wrong. To the degree that doing something under compulsion is worse than doing it willingly, to that degree law is worse than philosophy. For this reason do philosophy and do not take part in government. For it is better to know the means by which men are taught to do right than to know the means by which they are compelled not to do wrong.

CRATES (a Cynic), from a letter to his students

The purpose of punishment

NO ONE punishes a wrong-doer for the mere contemplation but on account of his wrong-doing, unless one takes unreasoning vengeance like a wild beast. But he who undertakes to punish with reason does not avenge himself for the past offence, since he cannot make what was done as though it had not come to pass; he looks rather to the future, and aims at preventing that particular person and others who see him punished from doing wrong again. And being so minded he must have in mind that virtue comes by training: for you observe that he punishes to deter.

PLATO, *Protagoras (324B)*

On litigation

YOU SEE, gentlemen ... we've got Acestor's disease – only in our case it's the other way around. He spends all his time, as an outsider, trying to find a way *in*; whereas we – respectable citizens, born of purest Athenian stock, and acting under no compulsion whatever – are clearing out. And why, you may ask, have we taken wing (on foot) from our native city? Well, it isn't that we've anything against the city as such: it's as grand and happy a place as ever a man paid a fine in. But there it is: the cicadas chirp away in the trees for a month on end, perhaps even two; but the Athenians yammer away in the law courts for the whole of their lives. Which is why you see us on the march, with our basket and our brazier and our myrtle, looking for a land without lawsuits, where we can settle down and live in peace.

ARISTOPHANES, *The Birds*

PERCEPTIONS OF
REALITY AND
THE IMMORTAL REALM

Man is the measure of all things.

PROTAGORAS

ON THE TRANSIENT NATURE OF LIFE

FOR MORTALS, neither grief,
nor wealth, nor the sparkling
night is stable, but all
disappear in an instant, and joy
or deprivation comes in turn to another.

SOPHOCLES, *Young Women of Trachis*

OH MOST dear son of Aigeus, only
the gods themselves never grow old and die.
Almighty Time obliterates all else.
The earth decays. The body's strength decays.
Faith dies and faithlessness instead grows strong.
The winds of change forever blow among
the company of friends and alliances of cities.
For some, it's now, for others, later on,
when friendship sours before it sweetens again.
So Thebes might now spend happy days
with you, but endless Time in constant cycles
breeds an endless stream of days and nights.

SOPHOCLES, *Oidipous at Kolonos*

LIKE THE generations of leaves, the lives of mortal men.
Now the wind scatters the old leaves across the earth,
now the living timber bursts with the new buds
and spring comes round again. And so with men:
as one generation comes to life, another dies away.

HOMER, *The Iliad Book 6*

ON THE NATURE OF THE UNIVERSE

THE FIRST principle is that nothing can be created from the non-existent; for otherwise any thing would be formed from anything without the need of seed ... Truly this universe has always been such as it now is, and so it shall always be; for there is nothing into which it can change, and there is nothing outside the universe that can enter into it and bring about a change....

Moreover, the universe consists of material bodies and void. That the bodies exist is made clear to all by sensation itself, on which reason must base its judgement in regard to what is imperceptible ... If that which we call 'void' and 'space' and 'the untouchable' did not exist, the particles of matter would have no place in which to exist or through which to move, as it is clear they do move.

In addition to these two, there is nothing that we can grasp in the mind, either through concepts or through analogy with concepts, that has real existence and is not referred to merely as a property or an accident of material things or of the void. Of material things, some are compounds, others are simple particles from which the compounds are formed. The particles are indivisible and unchangeable, as is necessary if all is not to

FIRST CAUSE?

ETERNITY

MATERIAL + VACUUM

be dissolved to nothing.... Therefore it is necessary that the first beginnings be <u>indivisible particles of matter</u>.

Moreover, the universe as a whole is <u>infinite</u>, for whatever is limited has an outermost edge to limit it, and such an edge is defined by something beyond ... Moreover, the universe is infinite both in the number of its atoms and in the extent of its void. If, on the one hand, the void were infinite and matter finite, the atoms would not remain anywhere but would be carried away and scattered through the infinite void, since there would be no atoms from without to support them and hold them together by striking them. If, on the other hand, the void were finite, there would not be room in it for an infinite number of atoms.

Finally, the number of worlds, some like ours and some unlike, is also infinite. For the atoms are infinite in number ... and they move through the greatest distances. The atoms suited for the creation and maintenance of a world have not been used up in the formation of a single world or of a limited number of them, whether like our world or different from it. There is nothing therefore that will stand in the way of there being <u>an infinite number of worlds</u>.

EPICURUS, from a letter to Herodotus

IF AN instrument, e.g. an axe, were a natural body, then its substance would be what it is to be an axe, and this would be its soul....

We must consider what has been said in relation to the parts of the body also. For, if the eye were an animal, sight would be its soul; for this is an eye's substance – that corresponding to its principle. The eye is matter for sight, and if this fails it is no longer an eye....

Just, then, as the cutting and the seeing, so too is the waking state actuality, while the soul is like sight and the potentiality of the instrument; the body is that which is this potentially. But just as the pupil and sight make up the eye, so in this case the soul and body make up the animal ...

Now the soul is in the primary way that by means of which we live, perceive, and think. Hence it will be a kind of principle and form, and not matter or subject.

Substance is so spoken of in three ways ... and of these cases one is <u>form</u>, another <u>matter</u>, and the third the product of the two; and of these matter is potentiality and form actuality. And since the product of the two is an ensouled thing, the body is not the actuality of soul, but the latter is the actuality of a certain kind of body.

And for this reason those have the right conception who believe that the soul does not exist without a body and yet is not itself a kind of body. For it is not a body, but something which belongs to a body, and for this reason exists in a body, and in a body of such and such a kind. Not as our predecessors supposed, when they fitted it to a body without any further determination of what body and of what kind, although it is clear that one chance thing does not receive another. In our way it happens just as reason demands. For the actuality of each thing comes naturally about in that which is already such potentially and in its appropriate matter. From all this it is clear that the soul is a kind of actuality and principle of that which has the potentiality to be such.

ARISTOTLE, *De Anima, Book II*

I⊤ IS not possible for one to rid himself of his fears about the most important things if he does not understand the nature of the universe but dreads some of the things he has learned in the myths. Therefore, it is not possible to gain unmixed happiness without natural science.

EPICURUS

On trying to change reality

THE INDIVIDUAL sensation ... does not depend on the reason and does not admit the recollection of an earlier sensation. It cannot set itself in motion but must be stirred by something external, and when so stirred it can neither add anything nor take anything away. There is nothing that can refute a sensation; for the sensation received by one sense cannot refute another of the same sense since both are equally valid, nor can a sensation received by one sense refute one received by another, since their subject matter is different. Reason cannot deny the truth of sensation, for all reason depends upon sensation; nor can one sense contradict another, for we pay equal attention to all. Also, the fact that our perceptions are in agreement guarantees the reliability of the senses. Our sight and our hearing are in agreement, as is also our feeling. Since sensation is valid, we must accept from things that we can perceive indications about things beyond the reach of the senses. Indeed, all our ideas are framed from sensations as we experience and compare them, recognise their similarities and combine them, not without the assistance of our reason.

EPICURUS, as expounded by DIOGENES LAERTIUS

IN PRAISE OF PROVIDENCE AND THE DIVINE

FROM EVERYTHING that happens in the universe it is easy to praise providence, if one has within him two things: the faculty of taking a comprehensive view of the things that happen to each person and a sense of gratitude. Otherwise, one man will not see the usefulness of what has happened, and another, even supposing that he does see it, will not be grateful for it. If god had made colours, but had not fashioned the faculty of sight, what good would it have been? None at all. Conversely, if he had made the faculty, but not made objects in such a way as to be amenable to the power of sight, in that case too, what good would it have been? None at all. And if he had indeed made both of these, but had not made light? Even then, it would have been of little use. Who, then, has fitted that to this and this to that? And who has fitted the sword to the scabbard, the scabbard to the sword – no one? But from the construction of manufactured objects we are accustomed to state that the work is certainly that of some craftsman, and has not been constructed at random. Does each of these, then, proclaim its craftsman, while visible things and sight and light do not? And the male and the female, and the passion of each one for intercourse with the other, and the faculty that uses the parts constructed for this purpose – do these not reveal their craftsman, too?

EPICTETUS, *Discourses I, chapter 6*

YOUR FAME, believe me, has reached the vaulting skies.
Fame like the flawless king's who dreads the gods
who governs a kingdom vast, proud and strong –
who upholds justice true, and the black earth
bears wheat and barley, trees bow down with fruit
and the sheep drop lambs and never fail and the sea
teams with fish – thanks to his decent, upright rule,
and under his sovereign sway the people flourish.

HOMER, *The Odyssey, Book 19*

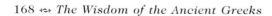

On the argument for the existence of an unmoved mover, or God

THERE IS something which is always moved through an uninterrupted motion, and this motion is circular (as is evident not merely by argument but as a matter of fact), and consequently the primary heaven will be eternal.

But there will then also be something that moved them. And since that which is moved and which also moves is an intermediate, it follows that there must be something that moves without being moved. This will be eternal, it will be a substance and it will be activation.

But there is in fact something that moves without being itself moved, existing in activation, and this does not admit of being in any way in another state. For spatial movement is the first of the changes, and of spatial movements rotation is the first. And it is this movement that the first mover produces. Its existence, then, is necessary, and in that it is necessary it is good, and it is in this way that it is a principle....

Our discussion has ... established that there exists a kind of eternal, unmoved substance that is separate from sensible things. It has further been shown that it is impossible for it to have any magnitude but that it is without parts and indivisible. The reason is that it is a source of movement for infinite time, and nothing that is finite has an infinite capacity. Hence, given that every magnitude is either finite or infinite, it could not have a finite magnitude. But neither could it have an infinite one, since there is quite generally no such thing as an infinite magnitude. It has also been shown that it is without affection or alteration, since all the other | UNALTERABLE motions are posterior to those in space. It should be quite clear, then, why the first mover is as we have said.

ARISTOTLE, *Metaphysics*, *Book Lambda*

GODS

THE GODS who hear us
Know what tempests
Tangle our lives, and bewilder our voyage
In their criss-cross winds.
But if there's a future
A huge tree can tower
From a tiny seed.

AESCHYLUS, *The Oresteia*

IT IS folly for a man to pray to the gods for that which he has the power to obtain for himself.

SELF-
RELIANCE

EPICURUS

(handwritten margin notes: "♀ ♂", "GOD .", "TRUTH . ONLY OBTAINED VIA PAIN")

WHAT IS good? Who is God? The mask
Of the great nameless.
Who can say anything about it?
I call God Zeus
And Zeus, or the greater one
Who wears Zeus like a mask for man to imagine,
Has given man this law:
The truth
Is to be melted out of our stubborn lives
By suffering.
Nothing speaks the truth,
Nothing tells us how things really are,
Nothing forces us to know
What we do not want to know
Except pain.
And this is how the gods declare their love.
Truth comes with pain.

AESCHYLUS, *The Oresteia*

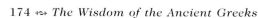

Of particular gods ...

THERE ARE two powers ... which are supreme
In human affairs: first, Demeter – the same goddess
Is also Earth; give her which name you please – and
  she
Supplies mankind with solid food. After her came
Dionysius, Semele's son; the blessing he procured
And gave to men is counterpart to that of bread:
The clear juice of the grape. When mortals drink their
  fill
Of wine, the sufferings of our unhappy race
Are banished, each day's troubles are forgotten in
  sleep.
There is no other cure for sorrow. Dionysius,
Himself a god, is thus poured out in offering
To the gods, so that through him come blessings on
  mankind.

EURIPIDES, *The Bacchae*

Gods controlling warfare

SO TYDIDES prayed and Athena heard his prayers,
put spirit in his limbs, his feet, his fighting hands
and close beside him winged him on with a flight of
    orders:
'Now take heart, Diomedes, fight it out with the
    Trojans!
Deep in your chest I've put your father's strength.
He never quaked, that Tydius, that great horseman –
what force the famous shieldsman used to wield.
Look, I've lifted the mist from off your eyes
that's blurred them up to now –
so you can tell a god from man on sight.
So now if a god comes up to test your mettle,
you must not fight the immortal powers head-on,
all but one of the deathless gods, that is –
if Aphrodite daughter of Zeus slips into battle,
she's the one to stab with your sharp bronze spear!'

HOMER, *The Iliad*, Book 5

Perceptions of Reality and the Immortal Realm ❧ 177

handwritten margin notes: ATHENA / DO NOT FIGHT THE GODS (ALLEGORY) / APHRODITE

On appealing to the gods

A RICH ATHENIAN was sailing with some other travellers. A violent tempest suddenly arose, and the boat capsized. Then, while the other passengers were trying to save themselves by swimming, the Athenian continually invoked the aid of the goddess Athena [patroness of the city], and promised offering after offering if only she would save him.

One of his shipwrecked companions, who swam beside him, said to him: 'Appeal to Athena by all means, but also move your arms!'

AESOP, *Fable 53*

EVEN THE gods themselves can bend and change,
and theirs is the greater power, honour, strength.
Even the gods, I say, with incense, soothing vows,
with full cups poured and the deep smoky savour
men can bring them round, begging for pardon
when one oversteps the mark, does something wrong.

HOMER, *The Iliad, Book 9*

THE GODS do indeed exist, for our perception of them is clear; but they are not such as the crowd imagines them to be, for most men do not retain the picture of the gods that they first receive. It is not the man who destroys the gods of popular belief who is impious, but he who describes the gods in the terms accepted by the many. For the opinions of the many about the gods are not perceptions but false suppositions.

POPULAR UNDERSTANDING IS WRONG

EPICURUS from the letter of Menoeceus

- 'GODS' UNDERSTOOD ALLEGORICALLY

LOVE IS a great Spirit ... for the whole of the spiritual is between divine and mortal ... Interpreting and transporting human things to the gods and divine things to men; entreaties and sacrifices from below, and ordinances and requitals from above: being midway between, it makes each to supplement the other, so that the whole is combined in one. Through it are conveyed all divination and priestcraft concerning sacrifice and ritual and incantations, and all soothsaying and sorcery. God with man does not mingle: but the spiritual is the means of all society and converse of men with gods and of gods with men, whether waking or asleep. Whosoever has skill in these affairs is a spiritual man; to have it in other matters, as in common arts and crafts, is for the mechanical. Many and multifarious are these spirits, and one of them is Love.

PLATO, *Symposium (203B)*

CONCERNING GODS there are some who say that the divine does not even exist, and others who say that it exists, but is inactive, negligent, and takes thought for nothing. A third group says it exists and takes thought, but only for great things in the heavens, not for anything on earth. A fourth group says that it takes thought for things on earth and for human affairs, but only in a general way, not for the interests of individuals. And there is a fifth group, among them Odysseus and Socrates, who say 'I cannot make a move without your noticing....'

Before all else, then, it is necessary to enquire about each of these opinions, whether it is soundly or unsoundly held. For if the gods don't exist, how can it be our goal to follow the gods? And if they exist, but take thought for nothing, how will this goal be sound? Or even supposing that they exist and take thought, if there is no communication from them to mankind, and by Zeus, to me personally, how again is the goal sound? The educated man, then, after considering all these things, submits his will to him who administers the universe, as good citizens do to the law of the state.

EPICTETUS, *Discourses I, chapter 12*

ATHEISTS

5 OPINIONS

SUBMISSION TO GOD

A PERSONAL GOD

Oracles and prophets

I'LL TELL you, this is my experience of prophets; you can expect nothing from them but silliness and lies. Shapes of *ABSURDITY* sacrifices, cries of birds – there's no truth in any of it, never was! Can birds do men any good? The very notion's foolish. Calchas saw his friends dying in battle for the sake of a phantom, yet he gave them neither word nor sign; no more did the Trojan Helenus – his city was sacked for nothing. You may say it was because the god did not wish them to speak. Then why do we consult prophets? Better ask the gods for blessing, after due offerings; and leave prophets alone. Prophecy was invented to entrap men with the promise of *FRAUD* success; no one ever got wealth without labour by studying sacrifices. The best oracle is care and common sense.

CARE + COMMON SENSE

EURIPIDES, *Helen*

THE QUEST FOR IMMORTALITY?

THEY ARE in love with what is immortal. Now those who are teeming in body betake them to women, and are amorous on this wise: by getting children they acquire an immortality, a memorial, and a state of bliss, which in their imagining they 'for all succeeding time procure'. But pregnancy of soul – for there are persons ... who in their souls still more than in their bodies conceive those things which are proper for soul to conceive and bring forth; and what are those things? Prudence, and virtue in general; and of these the begetters are all the poets and those craftsmen who are styled *inventors*.

PLATO, *Symposium (209C)*

THE LOVERS of knowledge are conscious that the soul was simply fastened and glued to the body – until philosophy took her in hand, she could only view real existence through the bars of a prison, not in and through herself, and she was wallowing in the mire of every sort of ignorance. This was her original state; and then ... philosophy saw the ingenuity of her prison – a prison built by lust so that a captive might be the principal accomplice in his own captivity – and took her in hand, and gently comforted her and sought to release her, pointing out that the eye and the ear and the other senses are full of deception, and persuading her to retire from them, and abstain from all but the necessary use of them, and be gathered up and collected into herself, bidding her trust only in herself and her own pure apprehension of pure existence, and to mistrust whatever comes to her through other channels and is subject to variation; for such things are sensible and visible, but what she sees in her own nature is of the mind and invisible.

PLATO, *Phaedo*

Of the universal nature of the divine

I F WHAT is said by the philosophers concerning the kinship of god and men is true, what other course remains for men than to do as Socrates did, never replying to anyone who asked him where he was from, 'I am Athenian', or 'I am Corinthian', but, 'I am a citizen of the world.' ... Anyone, though, who has come to understand the administration of the universe, has learned that the supreme and greatest and most inclusive government is the one composed of men and god. He knows that from god have descended the seeds of being, not only to his father or grandfather, but to all things born and engendered on the earth, but chiefly to rational beings, since they alone are equipped by nature to share in god's society, being entwined with him through reason. And why shouldn't he call himself a citizen of the world and a descendant of god? And why will he fear anything that happens?

EPICTETUS, *Discourses I, chapter 9*

On the future

H<small>E WHO</small> advises the young man to live well, the old man to die well, is foolish, not only because life is desirable, but also because the art of living well and the art of dying well are one ...

Remember that the future is neither ours nor wholly not ours, so that we may neither count on it as sure to come nor abandon hope of it as certain not to be.

E<small>PICURUS</small>, from the letter to Menoeceus

TRANSLATIONS USED

Aeschylus, *The Oresteia*, trans. Ted Hughes, Faber & Faber, 1999

Aesop, *The Complete Fables*, trans. Olivia and Robert Temple, Penguin, 1998

Aristophanes, *The Birds*, trans. David Barrett, Penguin, 1978

Aristophanes, *The Knights*, trans. Alan H. Sommerstein, Penguin, 1978

Aristotle, *De Anima*, trans. D. W. Hamlyn, Oxford University Press, 1968

Aristotle, *Ethics*, trans. J. A. K. Thomson, Penguin Classics, 1976

Aristotle, *Poetics*, trans. G. F. Felse, Harvard, 1967

Aristotle, *Politics*, trans. T. A. Sinclair, Penguin, 1962/1992

Aristotle, *The Metaphysics*, trans. H. Lawson-Tancred, Penguin Classics, 1998

Aristotle, *Topics*, trans. Robin Smith, Oxford University Press, 1997

Cynics, 'The Cynic Epistles', Abraham J. Malherbe, Scholars Press, 1977

Epictetus, *Discourses*, trans. Robert F. Dobbin, Oxford University Press, 1998

Epicurus, trans. R. M. Geer, Bobbs-Merrill, 1964

Euripides, *Ion, Helen* and *The Bacchae*, trans. Philip Velacott, Penguin, 1954, 1973

Euripides, *Medea*, trans. Michael Walton, Methuen Drama, 1998

Euripides, *The Phoenician Women*, trans. David Thompson, Methuen Drama, 1998

Homer, *The Iliad*, trans. Robert Fagles, Penguin, 1998

Homer, *The Odyssey*, trans. Robert Fagles, Penguin, 1996

Plato, *Apology, Phaedo* and *Ion*, trans. B. Jowett, Oxford University Press, 1871

Plato, *Protagoras, Gorgias, Meno, Larches, Lysis and Symposium*, trans. W. R. M. Lamb, Heinemann, 1924

Plato, *The Republic*, trans. F. M. Cornford, Oxford, 1941

Plotinus translations by John Gregory in *The Neoplatonists: a reader*, Routledge, 1999

Sophocles, *Electra*, trans. Michael Evans, Everyman, 2000

Sophocles, *Oidipous at Kolonos*, trans. Gregory McCart, Everyman, 2000

Sophocles, *Philoktetes*, trans. Graham Ley, Everyman, 2000

Sophocles, *Aias* and *Antigone*, trans. Michael Evans, Everyman, 1999

Sophocles, *Oidipous the King*, trans. Gregory McCourt, Everyman, 1999

Sophocles, *Young Women of Trachis*, trans. Graham Ley, Everyman, 1999

Sophocles, *Aleus's Sons*, trans. Michael Evans, Everyman, 2000

ACKNOWLEDGEMENTS

Pages 16 & 89, Aristotle (384–322 BC) (engraving) (b&w photo), Private Collection/Bridgeman Art Library. Pages 65 & 105, Ulysses and the Sirens, from 'The Odyssey' by Homer (mosaic) by Roman (3rd Century AD), Musee du Bardo, Tunis, Tunisia/Bridgeman Art Library. Pages 56, 136 & 184, School of Athens, detail of the centre showing Plato and Aristotle with students including Michelangelo and Diogenes, 1510–11 (fresco) (detail from 472) by Raphael (Raffaello Sanzio of Urbino) (1483–1520), Vatican Museums and Galleries, Vatican City, Italy/Bridgeman Art Library. Pages 73 & 149, screen panel depicting Aesop's fable 'The Fox and the Grapes', Savonnerie tapestry, mid 18th century, Mobilier National, Paris, France/Bridgeman Art Library. Pages 25, 97 & 165, mosaic of Dionysus riding a Leopard c.180 AD, House of Masks, Delos, Greece/Bridgeman Art Library. Pages 48, 132 & 176, facade of the Parthenon, built 447–432 BC (photo) by Callicrates and Ictinus (5th century BC), Acropolis, Athens, Greece/Bridgeman Art Library. Pages 28, 109 & 169, The Gods of Olympus, trompe l'oeil ceiling from the Sala dei Giganti, 1528 (fresco) by Giulio Romano (1492–1546) (workshop of), Palazzo del Te, Mantua, Italy/Bridgeman Art Library. Pages 40, 120 & 180, Jason seizing the Golden Fleece, Victorian book illustration, Private Collection/Bridgeman Art Library. Pages 61 & 140, The Trojan Horse, 1994 by Tamas Galambos (contemporary artist), Private Collection/Bridgeman Art Library.

Sin - in Greek?